FLORENCE NIGHTINGALE

FLORENCE NIGHTINGALE

A very brief history

LYNN McDONALD

First published in Great Britain in 2017

Society for Promoting Christian Knowledge
36 Causton Street
London SW1P 4ST
www.spck.org.uk

British Library Cataloguing-in-Publication Data
A catalogue record for this book is available from the British Library

ISBN 978–0–281–07645–1
eBook ISBN 978–0–281–07646–8

Typeset by Manila Typesetting Company
First printed in Great Britain by Ashford Colour Press
Subsequently digitally printed in Great Britain

eBook by Manila Typesetting Company

Produced on paper from sustainable forests

To my god-daughters,
Tricia Eakins
Antonia Butler
Laurena Clark

Contents

Chronology

their prevention; gives evidence on the subject
to the Royal Commission on the war

1859   First papers on hospital reform read at the
National Association for the Promotion
of Social Science; begins work on Royal
Commission on India

1860   (January) Publishes *Notes on Nursing: What It
Is and What It Is Not*; (June) the Nightingale
School opens at St Thomas's Hospital, London

1861   Nightingale Midwifery Ward and training
programme open at King's College Hospital,
London

1862   Sends advice on hospitals to the USA, for use in
the Civil War; first publication on India

1863   Publishes *Notes on Hospitals* as a full book;
sends paper 'How People May Live and Not Die
in India' to Social Science Congress

1865   First professional nursing in a workhouse
infirmary begins, in Liverpool,
with matron and nurses

1867   Sends brief on nursing to parliamentary committee on cubic space

1868   Nightingale matron and nurses begin at Sydney
Infirmary

1870   First publication in an Indian journal: 'On
Indian Sanitation', *Transactions of the Bengal
Social Science Association*

1870–1 Assists on relief for the Franco-Prussian War

1871   Publishes *Introductory Notes on Lying-in
Institutions*, on maternal mortality
post-childbirth

1872	Revises nursing programme at St Thomas's; begins nurse mentoring; first professional nursing at the Edinburgh Royal Infirmary with a Nightingale matron and nurses
1873	Three American nursing schools open using Nightingale system
1875	Nightingale matron and nurses begin at Montreal General Hospital, first professional nursing in Canada
1876	Publishes 'Trained Nursing for the Sick Poor' in *The Times* for promotion of district nursing (home visiting)
1877	First work on Indian famine relief
1879	Assists with nursing for the Zulu War
1880–1	Assists with nursing and hospitals for the Transvaal, or First Boer War
1882	Assists with nursing for first Egyptian campaign
1883	Publishes articles on nurse training and hospital nursing in Quain's *Dictionary of Medicine*
1884	Begins work with Lady Dufferin on female medical care for Indian women
1885	Assists with nursing for second Egyptian campaign
1887	Queen's Jubilee Nursing (home visiting) begins
1892	Publishes 'Hospitals' in *Chambers' Encyclopaedia: A Dictionary of Universal Knowledge*
1893	Sends paper, 'Sick-Nursing and Health-Nursing', to Chicago world conference
1894	Begins advising on nurse training in Italy

Part 1

THE HISTORY

1

Nightingale and the nineteenth century

Florence Nightingale (1820–1910) is perhaps still best known as the doyenne of the nursing profession. What is less familiar to most, however, is her contribution to the great ideas and causes of the nineteenth century. Nightingale became famous for her work during the Crimean War (1854–6), when she led the first team of British women to nurse in war. Then, during the rest of the century, she used the reputation she gained there to promote a series of great reforms. The establishment of professional nursing was only one of her achievements, and was always pursued in the context of broader public health concerns. She is still recognized for her contribution to hospital reform, from design to administration and the care of hospital employees. Her statistical innovations, in analysis and the presentation of data, however, also had an enormous impact: where would our annual financial reports be without the pie and bar charts she promoted?

Early life

Nightingale was born into a family of wealth and privilege – respectable, but not 'old money'. Her father, William E. Nightingale, had inherited a fortune, made from lead mining and smelting in Derbyshire, from a relation known as 'mad Uncle Peter', who would not leave his money to a closer female relative. W. E. Nightingale received a gentleman's education, in classics, at Trinity College, Cambridge. He owned two fine country houses, Lea Hurst in Derbyshire and Embley Park in Hampshire. He ran for Parliament once, just after the Reform Act of 1832 was passed and rotten and pocket boroughs were abolished. He was unwilling to bribe voters, however, and lost. Nightingale wished that he would take on such duties as chairing a hospital board, but he never did.

Nightingale's mother, Frances, was the daughter of a radical MP, William Smith, who had worked with William Wilberforce in the anti-slavery movement (Smith also supported the vote for Jews, Catholics and dissenters). Florence's parents regularly entertained MPs at Embley, and she was thus exposed to progressive ideas from her childhood. There were other progressive relatives too: Samuel Smith, a double uncle – brother of Frances Nightingale, he was married to the sister of William E. Nightingale – was an official in Parliament. Aunt Julia Smith was an abolitionist, while cousin Barbara Bodichon was a leading suffragist and promoter of women's employment. A Bonham Carter cousin was a Liberal MP.

Church and faith

Although there were Unitarians among her forebears, Nightingale was baptized in the Church of England and remained in it for life (the family attended the local parish church in Hampshire, a Methodist chapel when in Derbyshire). While she disliked the social conservatism of the established Church, much of its doctrine and its exclusion of women from serious roles, she had nothing good to say of Unitarianism. Roman Catholicism had more appeal, for it at least permitted women serious roles as nuns, but – unlike close friends such as Henry (later Cardinal) Manning, Elizabeth Herbert and Angelique Lucille Pringle, a Nightingale nurse, later matron of the Edinburgh Royal Infirmary and then St Thomas's Hospital – Nightingale was never tempted to convert. Indeed, as the Roman Catholic Church, under Pius IX, whom Nightingale met in Rome, became more conservative, she became more critical of it. She ridiculed, at least in private, Pius' declaration of the dogma of infallibility, saying: 'The pope is infallible because he says so. And we are to believe it because he is infallible who says so.'[1]

Despite her Protestant faith, Nightingale did not accept the conventional doctrine of eternal hellfire, which both Protestants and Roman Catholics applied to infants who died unbaptized. Good Friday was the most important day of the year, she held, and Christ's sacrifice – as a voluntary act – was sufficient for all. She thought that the portrayal of God as judge with weighing scales demanding that someone pay the penalty was false. God was wise, loving and benevolent. This was a consistent theme in her most philosophical work, *Suggestions for Thought*.

Nightingale nevertheless continued to read Catholic writers, and would keep in touch with the Sisters of Mercy in Bermondsey, who had nursed with her in the Crimean War. She recounted that its mother superior, Mary Clare Moore, a friend and the person who introduced her to the mystical writers, was the only Catholic she knew who never tried to convert her.

Movements within the Church of England, meanwhile, offered their adherents a range of perspectives and modes of worship. Nightingale knew the leader of the Anglo-Catholic movement, E. B. Pusey. At his request, she attended, as a nurse, the confession of a dying woman. She was a close friend of Benjamin Jowett, priest and master of Balliol College, Oxford, and a leader of the 'broad church' movement. Jowett was more heterodox than she, not believing in the survival of individual souls after death, let alone the resurrection of the dead; his notorious essay, 'On the Interpretation of Scripture', called for the Bible to be read and criticized like any other book.

Nightingale gave discreet support to such clerics when they came under attack for heresy; one such was Bishop John Colenso, although she found his theology unattractive. Ernest Renan's *Vie de Jesus* she read carefully and critically, although he had done nothing, she said, to 'show us the way'.[2] While a fervent believer in freedom of expression, she wondered about the consistency of ordained priests who made such heterodox statements despite signing the Church of England's Thirty-nine Articles. Jowett himself signed the Thirty-nine Articles twice, the second time to make peace after the outcry over his essay.

It is not often realized that Nightingale made an explicit commitment to serve Christ, thanks to reading *The Cornerstone*, by the American Congregational minister and educator Jacob Abbott.[3] In its opening chapter, the book states its intention

> to explain much of the elementary principles of the gospel of Christ as are necessary to supply the most pressing wants of a human soul hungering and thirsting after righteousness, and this gospel, the Bible assures us, cannot be understood unless the heart is willing to comply with its claims.

It urges the reader who has not yet asked for forgiveness to 'go to God before you proceed further'. This she did, recalling years later to Maude Verney, an evangelical relative by marriage, the 'American book which converted me in 1836. Alas! that I should so little have lived up to my conversion.'[4] Nightingale also read Abbott's *The Way to Do Good, or the Christian Character Mature*,[5] just before experiencing, in the form of a voice from God, her own 'call to service'. She interpreted that call – although the nature of her 'service' would change over time – as one to tend the sick and the poor.

Throughout her life, Nightingale would have respect for people of other religions. As a young woman travelling in Egypt, she once visited a mosque, dressed uncomfortably as a Muslim woman, with the intention of seeing how her 'fellow creatures' worshipped.[6] In an article for the *Journal of the National Indian Association*, she said that Hindus and Muslims supported their sick, old and infirm 'much better than we could do it for them'.[7]

Nightingale's India work would bring her into touch with Hindus, Muslims and Parsis. Conservative Hindus were a challenge for her – some had married as children and continued to support child marriage. Parsis, by contrast, were more progressive, denouncing child marriage, especially its worst concomitant, 'enforced widowhood', which entailed the punishment of girl widows for their husband's death.

Social and public health reform

At the age of 33, frustrated with her uneventful social life, Nightingale was provided by her father with an annuity enabling her to take up nursing, without the indignity of having to accept a salary. The hospital at which she first worked was not a workhouse, or even a general hospital, either of which she would have preferred, but the Establishment for Gentlewomen during Illness, an institution mainly for impecunious governesses. Its Ladies' Management Committee notably included Lady Cranworth (wife of the Lord Chancellor), Lady Canning (whose husband was soon to become Viceroy of India) and Elizabeth Herbert (wife of the Secretary at War).

Nightingale's artistically minded sister, Parthenope, later Lady Verney, was vehemently opposed to Nightingale accepting employment even at such a respectable hospital. She only changed her tune when the Crimean War brought celebrity to her sister's work. Sir Harry Verney, a Liberal MP, was a keen supporter of Nightingale's work and served for years as chair of her Fund Council, while Lord Palmerston, the Prime Minister who sent the Sanitary and Supply Commissions to reform the army hospitals and camps in that war, was a neighbour in Hampshire. Such excellent connections as these would help Nightingale in pursuing numerous causes, both when she went to nurse in the Crimean War and in her promotion of 'sanitary' reform after it.

The nineteenth century saw much progress on social reform, from the provision of compulsory state schools to the enlargement of the electorate and the granting of the vote to women at the municipal level. Married women were also given property rights and some access to higher education. Nightingale's interest in social reform focused largely on the relief of poverty; her efforts to bring about the reform of workhouses were truly pioneering, and many of them were turned into real hospitals, with quality care and even nursing schools. She looked to the abolition of the

Poor Law itself, setting out the principles for such a fundamental change and arguing in favour of providing asylums for the care of the aged and chronically ill, children and the mentally or physically disabled.

On the rise of trades unions, however, Nightingale sided with business, forecasting that the result would be job losses for workers. She remained a staunch Liberal, looking to the private sector to run the economy, although she wanted the state to provide jobs in times of economic downturn. Similarly, while she sought profound reform of the Poor Law, she never envisaged the extent of state provision for income security or care realized in the 'welfare state' of the mid-twentieth century.

The late nineteenth century was a time of great advance in statistics and quantitative analysis in the social sciences, especially in what would become sociology and political science. Before the establishment of academic departments dedicated to such subjects (the London School of Economics was founded only in 1895), statistical societies – the first of which, the Manchester Statistical Society, was instituted in 1833 – held conferences and published their transactions. Nightingale sent seven papers to the congresses of the National Association for the Promotion of Social Science, founded in 1857. She sent short papers on hospital reform to the 1860 congress of the International Statistical Congress in London, and on improved statistics on surgical outcomes to its next congress in Berlin in 1863.

One of Nightingale's earliest research efforts after finishing her Crimean War work was on mortality and illness in 'colonial schools and hospitals' – in other words, among indigenous people in Australia, Ceylon (Sri Lanka), southern Africa and Canada's Red River Settlement. Her research also took her into the issue of the disappearance of aboriginal peoples. Although the data was woefully inadequate – itself an indication of trouble – enough was available to show that rates of death and sickness were twice what they should be. She was unable, however, to persuade the Colonial Office to continue to monitor results, let alone make concerted improvements. She succeeded in getting public opinion interested – her papers received good coverage – but this did not lead to the serious action she hoped for. Nightingale would thereafter concentrate on India, where she had more influence on improving health and social conditions.

Nightingale typically worked on her research and policy development with a team of experts – doctors, engineers, statisticians and architects – so that the reports, books, articles and briefs produced were of high quality and lasting significance. The core principles of her causes, health promotion and high standards for the nursing profession, with her predilection for starting small and monitoring results, still make sense. Much of her writing is still relevant, even with the vast increase in knowledge in medical science, hospitals, public health and public administration.

British imperialism

The nineteenth century saw a vast expansion in the British Empire, justified by firmly held principles of imperialism. Nightingale was a reluctant, critical imperialist; while she saw the benefits of British rule in spreading western science and medicine, education and infrastructure, she firmly believed that British rule should benefit the people themselves, and was well able to see when it did not.

Nightingale's critical stance on imperialism can be traced back to her own birth in Florence. A substantial part of what is now Italy was then under Austro-Hungarian rule. During her travels in Europe with her family, Nightingale met exiled Italian independence leaders. Later, on a train trip with family friends, they passed Spielberg Prison, where other independence leaders were kept in harsh conditions. She told her family that she was 'glad to have seen' it: 'Imagine a place ten times more dreary, more dull, more hopeless than you ever imagined it before, and there is Spielberg.' Nothing, she said, could give them an idea of it: 'Dante and Milton could not do it, but the House of Austria is a greater than they. Spielberg is a greater creation than the *Inferno* with all its circles.' All were 'inferior to Spielberg as a habitation for the damned'.[8] As late as Good Friday 1889, Nightingale recalled to a relative the horrors of Spielberg Prison: Italy's great independence leaders had left their bones there, she said, or had come out 'after long years maimed and invalids for life'.[9]

Nightingale continued to identify with Florence and Italy for the rest of her life. She sent contributions and letters of support to independence causes. When Giuseppe Garibaldi, leader of the Risorgimento, the Italian independence movement, made a triumphant visit to England in 1864, he wanted to meet her. Alas, he resisted her attempt to convert him to the promotion of sanitary causes; she thought that, having gained the country from its Austrian occupiers, he should now begin the task of running it – but he, a general, preferred to stick to his guns.

Two years later, when the King of Italy was in Florence setting off on another battle, Nightingale's letter of support was read out to a cheering crowd. Asked to advise on organizing voluntary help for the wounded, she added stirring words to the rather dry advice she offered in response, wishing she could come to their aid herself, and saying she would give her life if it would hasten their success 'by half an hour'. She recalled the Sardinian contingent that fought with the Allies in the Crimea – their troops were 'glorious', their hospitals 'admirable', as the story was reported in the *Illustrated London News* of 16 June 1866. 'And what have not the Italians done since, in these eleven years? The work almost of eleven centuries.'

Nightingale would be a lifelong supporter of the underdog, consistent with her Liberal upbringing and her own youthful observations. She was sympathetic to Irish independence. A visit to Ireland in 1852 with family friends shows her paying her respects at Daniel O'Connell's grave, loving Dublin and finding Belfast too 'Orange'.[10] At a time when racist views were socially acceptable, Nightingale was an exception. Her own family's views on race were liberal. Sights on her travels such as that of an Egyptian slave market where Nubians, captured as girls, were sold (she noted the price), reinforced those values.[11]

When legislation was adopted in 1876 under the Conservative Prime Minister Benjamin Disraeli to make the Queen Empress of India, Liberals objected, and Nightingale herself never used the title. While India was regarded as the 'jewel in the crown' of the British Empire, Nightingale gave her time and energy to promoting public health and improving conditions for the country's poorest, the landless peasants. In India, famine prevention and relief took precedence over nursing – for, as she plainly put it, to be healthy one first of all has to be alive. Her first paper on India, dating to 1863, says as much in its title: 'How People

May Live and Not Die in India'. She was a strong sup-porter of local self-government in India, the first stage of what would become, after her lifetime, a full independence movement, and wrote a campaign letter for the first Indian national to win a seat in Parliament, Dadabhai Naoroji.

Nightingale did not win all her causes – far from it. But she learned to concentrate on those for which she had a fighting chance, where she could and did make a difference.

2

Faith in a secular world

Nightingale was a devout Christian, a Protestant. Thanks to her unusual respect for those of other churches and faiths, however, the tone of her writings would fit in easily with any contemporary interfaith organization. In notes on the 'progress' made through individuals in history, for example, she listed Buddha, Moses, Paul, Ignatius of Loyola, Francis of Assisi and Wesley.[1] It doubtless helped that her theology did not burden her with concern to save either Catholics, Jews, Muslims or Buddhists from hellfire.

Despite Nightingale's loyalty to the Church of England, she could appreciate much in Roman Catholicism. While 'the Church of England drove out Wesley', the Church of Rome would have made him 'a Saint John of Wesley', she wrote; the Quaker Elizabeth Fry would have become 'Saint Fry of the Prisons', and 'a Venerable Countess of Huntington' for Methodism. 'The Church of England', in contrast, 'would have ousted St Francis of Assisi, St Ignatius, St Teresa and a thousand others, men and women.'[2]

Nightingale's reading was wildly eclectic: the French Dominicans, the *Spiritual Exercises* of Ignatius of Loyola (in French), medieval and later mystics, popular religious novels, adventures of missionaries and the new critical writers like Ernest Renan. She was fond of Johann Gottfried von Herder's translation of the Psalms into German, which she copied out into her Bible.[3] She bought and handed out SPCK tracts. Such a range was unusual in her time, and would still be today. And she could be humorous in her comments. For example, she joked to her friend Benjamin Jowett that his Edinburgh lectures on Samuel Johnson were a '"tour de force" . . . as if St Paul had delivered a lecture on tents, or St John written a general epistle on fishing'.[4]

Nightingale translated and wrote commentaries on mystical writers, although they were never published. When her cousin, Rosalind Nash, offered them to the SPCK for publication in 1937, it declined on the grounds that better translations were available; although true, this misses the point of possible interest in her distinctive commentaries. As much of her manuscript as survived has been published in the *Collected Works* as 'Notes on Devotional Authors of the Middle Ages' (this was the title she used, although several of the mystics she wrote about lived in much later periods).[5]

The mysticism author Evelyn Underhill called Nightingale 'one of the greatest and most balanced contemplatives of the nineteenth century', although without citing any good source to this effect.[6] It might better be said that Nightingale believed in withdrawal for spiritual renewal, to recharge for the next campaign to repair the damage in God's world.

Missions and missionaries

Nightingale always admired those who took their message to the wider world, as had John Wesley and Ignatius of Loyola. She therefore supported the missionary societies of her time, although with some qualification, in their efforts to convert non-Christians, and particularly admired David Livingstone, 'one of the greatest men of our time'. When the Royal Geographical Society organized a rescue expedition for him, her letter of support, accompanied by a donation, or 'mite', as she called it, was read out at a Mansion House meeting. She wished Godspeed to the search to save him, 'or, if he is dead, to save his discoveries! If it cost £10,000 to send him a pair of boots, England ought to give it.'[7] After Livingstone's death, she wrote, at the request of his daughter, a tribute in which she called his work 'the most glorious . . . of our generation.' It 'opened those countries for God to enter in', she said, while 'he struck the first blow to abolish a hideous slave trade.' She likened him to Stephen, 'the first martyr'.[8]

On the other hand, she was troubled by the work of organizations such as the Zenana Mission (the name comes from the secluded quarters in which both Muslim and Hindu women lived), established to carry out evangelical work in the homes of Indian women. The mission also provided education and healthcare, including the care of women in childbirth, but this was the wrong time to seek their conversion, Nightingale thought. As she explained to Dr Henry Acland, who was about to give a speech on the mission, 'the hour of the native women's pain and danger' was not the time to urge upon them 'the greatest, the most momentous, of all changes to a native woman – one which involves the greatest sacrifice, viz., Christianity.' She named no names, but said that 'the most devoted Christian, one of the best lady doctors in India, says, it is "cruel."'

She advised Dr Acland further that he should emphasize that India was 'of all countries the one where you can least *dabble* with medicine'.[9] She had noted earlier a concern that mission agencies were obliged to compete, not in striving to reach the highest standard, but as to 'who can show the largest figures to the home society'.[10]

With the benefit of hindsight, Nightingale's cautions about conversion seem most appropriate. They would have been less well appreciated at the time.

Islam

When Nightingale, during her trip to Egypt, paid her visit to a mosque, she was told that it was 'an unprecedented act in Alexandria, where they are fanatical Muslims'. She was glad that she had done it, although 'I never felt so uncomfortable in all my life.' The required dress included a stripe of muslin over the nose 'like a horse's nose band', a stiff band 'which passes between your eyes and over and behind your head like a halter', a white veil and a 'black silk balloon' over the head, with loops for the wrists: 'you only breathe through your eyes.'[11]

Julius Mohl, a scholar of Persian and Arabic, was a close friend. German-born, and a professor at the Collège de France, he was married to an Englishwoman who was a friend of the Nightingale family. He told Nightingale that according to expert opinion, Islam was a dying force, an unreformed religion with waning attraction.

In 1898, Nightingale had a lengthy conversation with the then 23-year-old Aga Khan, founder of the All-India Muslim League, on a visit to London. He was 'a touching man, but you could never teach him sanitation', she said, the same complaint she had made of General Garibaldi in 1864. To the Aga Khan, 'sanitation is unreal and superstitious – and religion and spirituality is the only real thing . . . I never understood before how really impossible it is for an Eastern to care for material causes.'[12]

Christian faith and nursing

Nightingale's understanding of a personal mission, 'Here am I, Lord', was fundamental to her faith, as was God's assurance, 'Lo it is I'. The 'whole of religion,' she said, was in these 'four words of one syllable' in the Bible, 'what whole sermons cannot say so well.'[13] Many of the nurses Nightingale mentored were themselves ardent Christian believers, and a number told her that they, like her, had come to nursing on a 'call'. One of these was Agnes Jones, a committed evangelical who had pioneered nursing at the Liverpool Workhouse Infirmary; Nightingale's article on Jones's death ended by inviting the 'daughters of God' to take up the fight 'against vice and sin and misery and wretchedness' as Jones had.[14]

An insight into Nightingale's view of the relationship between nursing and faith can be gained from remarks she addressed to the matron of the Highgate Workhouse Infirmary in London. Paraphrasing a verse from the parable of the sheep and the goats (Matthew 25.36), she described nursing as one of the services Christ saw as being done for himself personally, as if 'he were once more on earth receiving them. When we are nursing the sick, we may actually be sure that he says to us, "I was sick and ye nursed me."'[15] At the request of Alice Fisher, the newly installed matron at Addenbrooke's Hospital, Cambridge, Nightingale sent a Christmas letter to be read to the nurses. Dated Christmas Eve, 1877, it said, 'Show that you have been with Jesus – don't be afraid of seeming unlearned and ignorant.' Nightingale acknowledged that she herself felt ignorant and unlearned 'every day of my life'.[16]

Among the many nurses who confided their doubts and anxieties to Nightingale, some consulted her about talking to patients about their beliefs. She was always wary: the nurse's task was patient care. Nurses could be 'religious with patients (but *not* in *preaching*), in dropping the word in season'.[17]

The clearest expression of the link between nursing and Christianity, however, can be found in the 'addresses' she prepared for students and nurses at the Nightingale School between 1872 and 1900. Nightingale's words would be read out by the chair or secretary of the Nightingale Fund Council at the annual meeting, and afterwards printed and circulated to former students and nurses. Although the school was secular, the addresses contained a sizeable dose of religion; there are frequent exhortations to Christian virtue and examples of heroic Christians, with some 200 biblical citations altogether. For example, her remarks to the nurses at Addenbrooke's about being with Jesus went into her 1878 address.

Some of the addresses seem to assume that all the nurses were Christians, even though Nightingale knew that they were not. In the first, delivered in 1872, she called 'Am I a Christian . . . the first and most important question for each one of us nurses. Let us ask it, each of herself, every day.'[18] In her address the next year, she suggested:

Feeling that God has made her what she is, she may seek to carry on her work in the hospital as a fellow worker with God. Remembering that Christ died for her, she may be ready to lay down her life for her patients.

She advised nurses to take some time for themselves alone: 'Christ was alone, from time to time, in the wilderness or on mountains. If *He* needed this, how much more must we?'

In 1874 she said, a nurse needed to 'nurse up in herself the "infant Christ," who should be born again in us every day'. Nurses needed a solid foundation for their work: 'this is what is called being *rooted and grounded in Christ*' (emphasis original). She asked, the following year, 'Can we hope, may we hope, that, at least some day, Christ may say even to our training school, as He did once to His first followers, "Ye are the salt of the earth"?' From that year, too, she wrote that nurses 'should wish to think (like Christ), that we have completed life, that we have finished the work which was given us to do, that we have not lost one of those, patients or nurses, who were entrusted to us'.

In her last address, in 1900, Nightingale called Christ 'the author of our profession'. Nurses honoured Christ 'when we are good nurses', and dishonoured 'Him when we are bad or careless nurses'. In the same address she contrasted Christianity with the Roman era, for while the Romans were 'superior in some ways . . . they had no idea of being good to the sick and weak. That came in with Christianity.' In an article published in Quain's *Dictionary of Medicine* (1883) there is another motivational example: 'A good nurse should be the Sermon on the Mount in herself.'[19]

The heavy moralizing tone of these pieces seems offputting now, and differs greatly from Nightingale's normal style. This inspirational component, however, was much in demand at the time, so that in years when Nightingale did not issue an address, matrons complained. A call to ever greater sacrifice and the achievement of higher standards was precisely what her audience wanted.

In Nightingale's day, and for decades afterwards, nurses in English hospitals attended chapel services and read prayers in the wards. Where the matron or tutor was so inclined, Bible studies might be offered on a voluntary basis. These practices ceased only with the secularization of English society and the entry of large numbers of nurses of other faiths into nursing.

Nursing the 'sick poor'

Nightingale was insistent that, at her school, care for the sick poor be the goal, without compromise in favour of paying patients. Elizabeth Fry's earlier nursing institute had served private patients, whose fees subsidized nursing for those who could not pay. Nightingale wanted no such arrangements. Experience taught that, wherever private patients were admitted, it was they who received the best care. At Johns Hopkins University Hospital, the medical chief, William Osler, wrote to the matron, Isabel Hampton (later Robb), suggesting placing 'only the senior or the graduates' in them.[20] In a marked difference from any of Nightingale's publications, Hampton Robb's nursing text-book, not so incidentally, includes in its title a reference to the care of private patients: *Nursing: Its Principles and Practice for Hospital and Private Use.*

Nightingale had been consistent in this focus on the poorest since her pre-Crimea visits to workhouse infirmaries. Pondering her goal on her return from the war, she said it was to nurse in 'the poorest and least organized hospital in London'.[21] Workhouse infirmaries would remain a priority throughout her life. Although there is no known link between the two, the commitment could be seen as an early version of the 'preferential option for the poor' that would appear in Roman Catholic social teaching in the 1970s.

Love of nature, Franciscan spirituality

Nightingale was fond of the Psalms, in many of which rivers and mountains are depicted as praising God. A countrywoman, in her youth she was a keen observer of the time flowers bloomed and the numbers of birds. Even in her later years, when as a result of sickness she was seldom able to get outside, she continued to take delight in what she could see from her window overlooking the garden at the Dorchester Hotel in Park Lane.

Nightingale's love of nature places her in the tradition of St Francis of Assisi: 'There is nothing makes my heart thrill like the voice of birds, much more than the human voice.' They were 'angels calling us with their songs'.[22] At the end of the 1882 campaign in Egypt, she remarked, 'Every little bird seems to sing its praise for this great mercy.'[23] A later letter describes birds 'whispering at dawn their prayers to God'.[24] An American Catholic theologian commented on her Franciscan love 'for all of God's creatures'.[25]

She also wrote serious letters on animal welfare, such as one to the secretary of the Society for the Prevention of Cruelty to Animals about the trapping of birds, the prizes given to those who caught the most, and the resulting decline in bird numbers: 'one singing or small bird is scarcely seen where there used to be hundreds.'[26]

A letter to her brother-in-law, written on her seventieth birthday, sums up her love of nature:

I never see a soap bubble when I am washing my hands without thinking how good God was when He invented water and made us invent soap – He thought of us all and thought how he could make the process of cleansing delightful to our eyes so that every bubble should show us the most beautiful colours in the world . . . Some Scotch doctor says, wait for the buds and the birds and trust in God. So I scarcely ever see that lovely thing, a bird, without thinking it teaches me to trust in God.[27]

3

The Crimean War

The Crimean War of 1854–6 would soon be judged to have been a mistake. Its death rates were enormous, its ostensible causes were not its real causes, and its (negligible) results were soon reversed. Its origins lie partly in the desire of Britain to prevent Russia from threatening its route to India. The French, however, were the main instigators of the war, and the best prepared for it: the newly proclaimed Emperor of France, Napoleon III, had political ambitions and was keen to match the exploits of his putative uncle, Napoleon Bonaparte. Asserting Roman Catholic control over the sites of the Holy Land, in place of the Orthodox Church, an ostensible cause, was good politics back home.

The Ottoman Empire and Russia declared war against each other in October 1853. Britain and France issued their own declarations of war on Russia in March 1854 and began sending troops to 'the East' in April, initially to Scutari, on the Asian side of the Bosphorus, opposite Constantinople (now Istanbul). The armies were then sent to Varna, Bulgaria, close to the Russian army 'south of the Danube'. Britain feared the Russians might advance further, into vulnerable Turkey, the 'the sick man of Europe'. When Russia, however, moved its troops back north of the Danube, the most serious cause of the war was removed.

Taking Sebastopol then became the goal of the Allied forces. They invaded Crimea in early September 1854, landing without opposition. The three battles of that autumn were all won by the Allies: the Alma on 20 September; Balaclava (in response to a surprise Russian attack) on 25 October; Inkerman on 5 November. The Allies failed to take their objective, however, and settled in for a lengthy siege 'before Sebastopol', as newspaper dispatches put it, entirely unequipped for the brutal cold.[1]

The British Commander-in-Chief was Lord Raglan, famous for losing his arm (as a result of which his tailor designed the original raglan sleeve) at the Battle of Waterloo in 1815. Raglan served as the Duke of Wellington's Secretary, and was to succeed him as commander of the forces without ever having commanded in the field. The British had not fought an army of comparable strength and technology since Waterloo. They were badly prepared for the war, and the blame has to be allocated to the Cabinet. Incompetent as the War Office and its Army Medical Department undoubtedly were, they could hardly have prepared effectively for a winter siege with the vague instructions given them by those in charge of government.

Massive illness and death from disease had begun even while the troops were in Bulgaria. The area was riddled with infection, and cholera was rampant; no cure for it was known, while the standard treatments – emetics and purging, which dehydrate the body – did more harm than good. (Not until the mid-twentieth century was oral rehydration found to be highly effective, radically reducing the incidence of death.)

The death rates among all the armies were appalling, and were overwhelmingly the result of disease, not wounds. The French Commander-in-Chief, Marshal St Arnaud, died before the first battle, Raglan in June 1855. Doctors and nurses died, as did officers and men, railway workers and labourers.

That the British were well behind the French in the care of the sick and wounded was first revealed in British newspapers in September 1854. This was the first war in which correspondents filed stories by wire, although no direct connection was yet available, so that there was still a delay of ten days or so before news appeared. It was such coverage that made the British government decide to send women nurses – they had considered this novelty earlier, but had rejected it. 'Why don't the British have Sisters of Charity?' was the cry, and Florence Nightingale, among a group of Roman Catholic and Anglican nuns, 'lady' volunteers and paid nurses – in practice, these last were the most useful – arrived in Turkey on 5 November 1854, the day of the Battle of Inkerman. Wounded troops soon began landing at their hospitals, joining the large number already there thanks to illness and the two earlier battles.

Nightingale's headquarters: the Barrack Hospital, Scutari

Nightingale was first stationed at the Barrack Hospital. This was, literally, a barracks, given by the Turks to the British for medical use. It was large and badly ventilated, had no operating theatre or laundry, and the plumbing did not work. Dr Menzies, the principal medical officer, did not want women nurses and made life difficult for them. Before long, however, he was sent home for general incompetence and for demanding bribes from suppliers.[2] His successor, Dr McGrigor, and most doctors there and elsewhere, were pleased to have the nurses.

Nightingale and her nurses quickly made a difference. Medication, clothing and hospital supplies often failed to arrive at the right place; supplies needed at Scutari, for example, were mistakenly sent on to Balaclava, to return only weeks later. Much of Nightingale's time was therefore spent in making up for missing supplies, establishing laundries and kitchens.

Having been seen at night going through the long corridors of the Barrack Hospital, Nightingale soon became known in the media as 'The Lady with the Lamp'. She was often accompanied by a young Irish soldier, who had enlisted at the age of 15, fell ill at Varna and was shipped out to the Crimea, to be sent on to Scutari without ever seeing a day's battle. He would carry the lamp for her so that she could take down the last letters of dying soldiers.

During the war, Nightingale herself both nursed and supervised the nursing in a growing number of hospitals. However, her most effective contribution was the establishment of laundries and kitchens. Laundries, equipped with hot water and drying machines – the latter sent by Charles Dickens and Britain's wealthiest woman, Angela Burdett-Coutts – provided clean bedding and clothing for men who arrived covered with vermin and excrement. Scurvy was a serious problem, although one for which the means of prevention, citrus fruits and vegetables, had been discovered some 50 years earlier; the kitchens, organized by a volunteer chef, Alexis Soyer, produced nutritious food, including vegetables and rice, for soldiers otherwise confined to salt meat, hard biscuit and rum.

Bedside nursing cannot work if the air and water are polluted, dead animals decompose in the water supply, the graveyard is too close, faeces flow across the floor from plugged toilet holes and ventilation is lacking from the very design of the building. All these matters took particular, complex, efforts to address. Nightingale learned that any serious mistake or lack in the requisites for health cost lives. Yet the Barrack Hospital had been inspected and approved, with minor requirements for alteration, by the inspector general of hospitals, Dr (later Sir) John Hall, Nightingale's nemesis. Reports by medical officers of the plugged holes that were used as toilets went unheeded.

Essential major renovations were not begun until March 1855, thanks to the arrival of the Sanitary Commission. Sent out from England by the Prime Minister, Lord Palmerston, rather than by the complacent War Office or its Army Medical Department, the Commission was led by the Edinburgh-educated Dr John Sutherland, who had learned 'sanitary science' in Liverpool, the city that pioneered preventive health measures in the UK. Its second member was Robert (later Sir Robert) Rawlinson, a civil engineer. 'Nuisance inspectors' from Liverpool, with hired Turkish help, shovelled out the muck and did the necessary rebuilding.

Dr Sutherland would become Nightingale's closest colleague in her post-Crimea reform work, while Rawlinson became her water expert. Other members of her team were also old Crimea hands, united on a mission to ensure that such death rates did not recur. The lessons learned from that experience would influence Nightingale's approach to nursing and hospital reform from then on.

In March 1855, Nightingale had a visitor at the Barrack Hospital. The Jamaican businesswoman Mary Seacole would become famous for her officers' bar and restaurant near Balaclava, the so-called 'British Hotel'. Then en route to the Crimea, Mrs Seacole spent a day visiting the hospital, where there were patients she had known in Jamaica. She then asked Nightingale for a bed for the night. She recorded

Nightingale's amicable words in her fine memoir: 'What do you want, Mrs Seacole – anything that we can do for you? If it lies in my power, I shall be very happy.'[3]

Post-war analysis: what went wrong and how to prevent it

Nightingale undoubtedly saved more lives by the work she did after the war than during it. Soon after her return to England in August 1856, the last patient having been discharged, she was summoned to Balmoral Castle to meet the Queen, the Prince Consort and the Secretary of State for War, Lord Panmure. He commissioned her to write, within six months, a 'précis' on the war hospitals; what she produced was an 853-page document, printed, but never actually published, in late 1858. This was her 'confidential report', which she sent privately to a sizeable number of influential people, with strict instructions not to circulate it.[4] She duly gave a full account of what had gone wrong during the campaign, and what administrative changes were needed to avoid such errors in the future. She was ill by this time and wanted to make sure that a comprehensive statement was issued, not only of the mistakes made, but of those brave enough to report defects, and with what result. Just after her report was printed, the War Office made correspondence available that proved to be so devastating that she spliced in whole new sections, and had the report reprinted.

Nightingale in the same period also worked behind the scenes on the official Royal Commission on the war, chaired by her friend Sidney Herbert, who as Secretary at War had sent her to the conflict in the first place. She briefed witnesses and submitted her own written evidence (by convention, only men spoke before public bodies such as a royal commission).[5]

Nightingale's confidential report and that of the Royal Commission were both forward-thinking documents, emphasizing how things might be done differently in the future. Nightingale's report also laid blame and named names, but gave far more space to getting the system right. There is much material on civilian hospitals, for, whether civilian or military, the sanitary requirements of a hospital are the same. Nightingale would draw substantially on this analysis in formulating the ideas on nursing and hospitals laid out in her next publications.

In her own analysis, and that for the Royal Commission, Nightingale worked closely with Dr William Farr, Superintendent of Statistics at the General Register Office and a leading medical statistician. They were an excellent team: he was more experienced than she in statistics, but he lacked her direct experience and bolder vision. His office prepared the statistics (although secondary sources often claim that Nightingale collected them herself, an impossible task in the circumstances). Yet clearly she contributed much, for the charts and tables they produced together are better than any he had ever created on his own. He nominated her to become the first woman fellow of the Royal Statistical Society. Strong, quantitative documentation would be a feature of her work from then on.

The people Nightingale met during the Crimean War would become friends and allies for life. The fame she gained, moreover, gave her an entry to the highest circles of politics, royalty and science, in her own country and around the world. She would use it to great effect to press for social reform and the improvement of public health.

4

Founding a new profession

Nursing – that is, trained, skilled attendance on the sick – was a nineteenth-century invention, and it was Florence Nightingale's. It is ironic that the profession should have originated in a country whose 'nurses' were disreputable and slatternly, typified by comic characters in Charles Dickens's novel *Martin Chuzzlewit* such as Sairey Gamp and Betsy Prig. Roman Catholic hospitals in Continental Europe, by contrast, already had nuns who gave devoted service to the sick, as did Protestant deaconesses, although neither were trained.

Nightingale had obtained ward experience in both the Kaiserswerth Deaconess Institute in Germany and with nuns in Paris, although she had reason to fault their standards of hygiene. Many doctors before Nightingale had seen the need for a skilled attendant to be available when they left the patient, especially in cases of fever. Given the lack of training programmes, some doctors gave informal training to a trusted nurse, who would then look after his patients. An Irish physician advised other doctors in 1843 not to undertake any fever case without 'a regular fever nurse', although how to obtain one he did not say.[1]

It was Nightingale's genius to see that the remedy to problems of poor care and hygiene lay in a training programme, to be offered in a hospital that could provide an adequate range of cases for teaching purposes. Nightingale had hoped to gain such experience in Salisbury with a doctor and family friend, but her family did not allow it. During the Crimean War, she had learned to dress wounds from the admirable Mrs Roberts, one of the responsible nurses from the bad old days at St Thomas's, who was by then retired. However, in no British hospital was there any organized training or examination of nurses; no one was responsible for seeing that it was properly done.

A 'Nightingale Fund', raised late in the war in her honour, enabled Nightingale to found the first nurse training school in the world. Meetings were held to raise funds not only in the UK but in Australia, New Zealand, France and India, those in the colonies typically being chaired by the governor or a bishop. Subscription lists were announced, concerts and theatrical performances organized to raise money. Banks and post offices lent their facilities to accept donations. Newspapers gave generous coverage to the fund-raising projects and some also discussed how the money might best be spent. All of this helped to gain Nightingale an international reputation, and widely circulated her goal of making nursing a serious profession, an art and a science. The school opened in June 1860 at St Thomas's Hospital in London, and a midwifery nurse training programme began the following year at King's College Hospital. Despite her own faith, Nightingale's school was secular. Few Roman Catholics attended it in its early decades, but many from non-Anglican denominations did.

The matrons of both hospitals had already begun to improve nursing practice. Although untrained and without hospital experience, Sarah E. Wardroper, appointed matron at St Thomas's in January 1854, was relatively well educated, a doctor's widow who needed to support her four children.

She set higher standards of conduct for nurses, improved their pay and working conditions, and gained better applicants as a result. Although she took no interest in training, she led the nursing at St Thomas's until her retirement in 1887, and assisted greatly in sending out staffs to other hospitals. Mary Jones, matron of King's and an Anglican nun, both had hospital experience and was keen on training. She, however, quit her order (and nursing itself) in 1868.

Nightingale left the running of the school to Sarah Wardroper in its early years, taking a more active role only when problems emerged in 1871. From 1872 on, she met many of the pupils at the end of their year's training, and kept in touch with those who took on matrons' or ward sisters' positions, either at St Thomas's or elsewhere. The training was conducted largely by apprenticeship, at the bedside, but was augmented by a small number of lectures given by doctors. This model would be followed in other nursing schools for many years.

Nightingale's mission for nursing was based on her faith, and this was the motive, too, of many other early nursing leaders. Nurses of faith were aware that Nightingale and other Christian nurses prayed for them. Sybil Airy, matron at the Citadel Hospital, Cairo, told Nightingale, when reporting on the many deaths among cholera patients and orderlies, that she was sure the prayers offered at home would keep morale up, as the sisters were 'well and in capital spirits'.[2]

British hospitals had Church of England chapels and chaplains, and the latter sometimes accompanied troops on foreign assignments.

Nightingale published her most famous book, *Notes on Nursing: What It Is and What It Is Not*, in 1860, six months before her school opened, but with no intention of its becoming a textbook. The book reflected what she had learned in the defective hospitals of the Crimean War, as can readily be seen from the chapter titles. Chapter 1 was on 'Ventilation', presumably because the lack of it was a major cause of death. Chapters on 'Bedding', 'Light' and 'Cleanliness of rooms and walls' all reflected the lack of these things at the Crimean hospitals. There were two chapters on food: 'What Food', on its content – poor diet was a major cause of illness during the war – and 'Taking Food', on serving food in a form that patients were able to consume before intravenous feeding became an option. 'Personal cleanliness' included Nightingale's first advocacy of frequent handwashing, which is still regarded as the single most effective means of preventing cross-infection.[3] Here the requirement was simply to wash with soap – the 'face, too, so much the better'. Disinfectants, which became important in her later writings, were not specified.

The chapter on 'Observation', unlike most of the others, concerned itself with the nurse's responsibility to the doctor, stressing what he needs to learn from her of a case. Chapter 2, on the other hand, 'Health of houses', was aimed not at the professional nurse but at homemakers responsible for the family's health. The book, in other words, had multiple purposes. Its unifying theme, however, was the importance of the biophysical environment, of the nurse's responsibility to ensure clean air, light, water, adequate space, nutrition, quiet and so on. It was translated into many languages and used throughout the world.

The 'sanitary' movement was already well under way when Nightingale came of age, and she knew several of its leaders, notably Edwin Chadwick. A lawyer by training,

Chadwick had served on government-appointed commissions to examine the plight of factory children, the working of the Poor Law and sanitary reform. Nightingale's most important collaborator, Dr John Sutherland, had been an inspector in Liverpool. Dr John Simon (of whom she had decidedly mixed views) was at the General Board of Health in London, while Dr Farr was at the General Register Office.

'Sanitary science', or what would now be called public health, was not then taught in any medical school or university department. Concerned citizens, including doctors, formed societies to pursue this interest. The Manchester Statistical Society fostered early work on hospital reform from its foundation in 1833, as did the London Statistical Society, later the Royal Statistical Society, which emerged the following year. The National Association for the Promotion of Social Science, modelled on the slightly earlier British Association for the Advancement of Science, was founded in 1857 by Dr George Woodyatt Hastings. the son of the doctor who founded the British Medical Association. The association's annual Social Science Congresses included a forum on public health to which reform-minded doctors and other activists could give papers; these were then published in the association's journal. The meetings attracted large audiences, sometimes of a thousand or more – including a number of women who both attended and presented papers – and gained considerable newspaper coverage.

Nightingale sent seven papers to the congress, beginning with the second in 1858. This first paper, on the defects apparent in contemporary hospitals, was well supported by colleagues in attendance. Prince Alfred, Duke of Edinburgh, the Queen's second son, attended the 1863 session in Edinburgh to hear her paper 'Sanitary Statistics of

Colonial Schools'. Discussion of it led to the adoption of a resolution, proposed by James Heywood, later President of the Royal Statistical Society, to represent the importance of her findings to the Colonial Office, with the request that it continue to collect data. This was however to no avail.

Journals on public health were later in coming: first published in the United States in 1873, *The Sanitarian, A Monthly Magazine Devoted to the Preservation of Health, Mental and Physical*, was edited by Agrippa Nelson Bell, an American naval surgeon; and, in the UK, in 1874, *The Sanitary Record: A Journal of Public Health* was founded by Ernest Hart, who also edited the *British Medical Journal.*

Workhouse infirmary nursing

It was Nightingale's vision – unique at the time – that nursing at workhouse infirmaries should be of the same quality as that provided in regular hospitals. Workhouse infirmaries were then the only recourse for the vast majority of the population, probably 80 per cent or more, when seriously ill. Bed sharing was common, while the infirmaries had no resident doctors, only visitors who had to pay, out of their stipend, for any drugs they prescribed. Nor were there any trained nurses, only 'pauper nurses', inmates who were not themselves ill, and who were even more notorious for stealing their patients' gin than the regular hospital staff.

These defects were well known and attracted various efforts at remedy. Doctors formed the Metropolitan Poor Law Medical Officers' Association, which ensured that prescriptions were paid for. Yet some workhouses economized by halving the prescription, or giving only a placebo.

In 1856 Dr Henry Bence Jones, at the request of the Poor Law Board, produced a report on the St Pancras Workhouse Infirmary. It painted a picture of overcrowding, bad smells, patients left on the floor as a result of bed shortages, and sickness among both patients and staff. When his plea for government action went unheeded,[4] Jones encouraged Nightingale to take up the issue.

She was not able to do so until her own school was well under way. It was only in 1865, thanks to Liverpool philanthropist William Rathbone, that a three-year experiment in trained care first took place in a workhouse infirmary. It proved to be unequivocally successful. The Liverpool workhouse authorities saw patients get better and get out, and were keen to continue.

An unnecessary death, caused by the lack of nursing care, at the Holborn Workhouse Infirmary prompted an inquiry in 1866. With the timely example of the Liverpool infirmary to hand, Nightingale seized the opportunity to press for wholesale reform in the London workhouse infirmaries. It took legislation, in the form of the Metropolitan Poor Bill of 1867, to make the introduction of paid nursing possible in London. Nightingale had hoped for nursing to become a requirement, but the bill was a compromise measure, permitting, but not requiring, the employment of trained nurses. Her aspirations were well beyond anything even her fellow Liberals could contemplate, and the replacement of the Liberal government by a Conservative administration did not help. Reforms were only introduced when boards of guardians – usually those with a progressive chair – sought them.

The act also established, under the Metropolitan Asylums Board, a new category of institution. Specifically, it increased the space allocated to each patient and established separate 'fever hospitals' for infectious cases. It also established dispensaries separate from workhouses and schools for children. These too Nightingale encouraged, and some were staffed by trained nurses and matrons from her school. In a sense they were prototypes for the NHS: publicly funded, not charitable institutions, but physically separate from existing workhouses.

The philanthropist Louisa Twining did much to improve the conditions in workhouses. Having herself visited the Strand Union Workhorse and raised her concerns in public, she founded the Workhouse Visiting Society in 1858. Then, in 1879, after the success in Liverpool and elsewhere, she launched the more ambitious Association for Promoting Trained Nursing in Workhouse Infirmaries. With the example of Liverpool before them, doctors too raised their sights. Ernest Hart and Francis Anstie – the latter, for Nightingale, the 'best of the workhouse doctors' – joined with Joseph Rogers to form the Association for the Improvement of London Workhouse Infirmaries in 1866. After initially focusing on the metropolis, they expanded the remit of their organization to include workhouse infirmaries throughout the country.

Rogers was the only workhouse doctor to publish an account of a specific institution, a sorry tale of pauper nurses who stole wine and brandy from their patients, and were intoxicated by the afternoon.[5] In his workhouse, 446 people shared 332 beds; the cubic space per patient was half that provided for prisoners, one-quarter of that allocated to soldiers in barracks. There was no way to separate acute, chronic, dying and infectious patients.[6] Workhouse doctors themselves could not agitate, however, as they were vulnerable to dismissal by the governors. Dr Rogers himself was dismissed from his position at the Strand Union Workhouse.

Devolving from her faith, the cause of workhouse reform was always close to Nightingale's heart. As she told Edwin Chadwick:

> Sickness, madness, imbecility and permanent infirmity are general inflictions affecting the entire community (mainly, too, brought about by the wretched sanitary state of our streets), and are not, like pauperism, to be kept down. The sick or infirm or mad pauper ceases to be a pauper when so afflicted.[7]

She said much the same thing to her father the next year, adding: 'Love to mankind ought to be our one principle in the Poor Law, not philanthropy – philanthropy is the biggest humbug I know.'[8] The reform of workhouse nursing and the upgrading of workhouse infirmary buildings would become an important part of Nightingale's legacy.

5

Safer hospitals

Quality nursing requires good hospitals, efficiently run in the interest of patient care, easy to keep clean and, most importantly, safe. Hospital conditions in Nightingale's time were risky for nurses and patients alike. Nightingale would hold that the level of deaths among nurses was a test of a hospital's quality – she included a table on nurse deaths in *Notes on Hospitals*. It is no coincidence that she published studies on the improvement of hospitals before writing her famous *Notes on Nursing*, 1860. The defects of the Crimean War hospitals had been all too evident, up to 40 per cent of those admitted dying in the worst hospital in its worst month. Even London teaching hospitals had death rates of roughly 10 per cent of admissions when Nightingale took up the cause.

That defective hospital buildings were responsible for such high death rates was argued by a Scottish-born surgeon then practising in Manchester. John Roberton, in 'On the Defects, with Reference to the Plan of Construction and Ventilation, of Most of our Hospitals', a paper delivered to the Manchester Statistical Society in 1855, did not then advocate what was known as the pavilion model as the remedy, but this would soon become his preference, as it would for Nightingale and other hospital reformers. The great advantage of the pavilion model was that each ward, or pavilion, was in effect its own hospital. Hospitals of the time typically had long corridors, often with double wards on each side, so that the air circulated among hundreds of people without being removed. In contrast, the wards of pavilion hospitals were narrow, with windows facing each other. The number of people (about 30 patients, plus doctors, nurses and cleaners) sharing the same air space was smaller than in the regular design, thus reducing the risk of cross-infection. The pavilion model also specified spatial separation of toilet areas, with separate ventilation. The laundry was relegated to a separate building, as was the mortuary or 'deadhouse'. Offices for administration, mainly for the protection of non-clinical staff, also had to be physically separate from the sick pavilions.

The advantages of the pavilion model were obvious: maximization of ventilation and, if sited correctly, sunlight, with minimal chances for cross-infection from 'hospital gangrene' or a 'hospital atmosphere'.

The French were the pioneers of the model, perhaps because of the very high death rates at their hospitals. Hospital design, however, was not their only fault, for they used large beds, for from four to six patients – a sure way to spread disease. Dr Jacques René Tenon had opened up the subject of hospital reform with five 'memoirs', or short papers, delivered to the Academy of Science in 1788, and afterwards to be sold for the benefit of Paris hospitals. He had visited early English naval hospitals built on the pavilion model – Christopher Wren's Greenwich Hospital was, and remains, a fine example – although the style had been chosen for its architectural grandeur rather than for any advantage of hygiene. In maternity hospitals, the subject of one Tenon memoir, he reported infant death rates of one in five, and noted that women who gave birth at home rarely suffered puerperal fever, even in the poorest of circumstances.[1]

Nightingale and her colleagues sent doctors and architects to France to view some early examples of the pavilion model. A favourite was the Lariboisière, opened in 1854 and still in operation today, conveniently located close to the Gare du Nord. Nightingale faulted it, however, for its artificial ventilation, which facilitated cross-infection. She had allies from the beginning: not only Dr Roberton in Manchester but the editor of a major architectural journal, *The Builder*. George Godwin published her critiques of faulty buildings and her advocacy of the pavilion model.

The Herbert Hospital in Woolwich, which opened in 1865, was the military exemplar of the pavilion model. The Leeds General Infirmary, in 1869, was the first civil hospital to be built on the pavilion model in the UK. Its architect was one Nightingale favoured, and she offered her advice. However, it was the new St Thomas's Hospital, opened in 1871 on the opposite bank of the Thames from the Houses of Parliament, that became the favoured example. Soon doctors and architects from around the world – including Dr John Shaw Billings, who designed Johns Hopkins University Hospital – would be visiting these as well as the French hospitals. The Herbert Hospital was eventually closed; the buildings, however, still stand, having been renovated as luxury apartments under the name Royal Herbert Mansions.

Naturally, Nightingale promoted the pavilion model for workhouses as well as for civil and military hospitals. In fact, the very first pavilion hospital in the UK – Crumpsall, near Manchester, built in 1855 – was a workhouse infirmary; another, at Blackburn, had been planned earlier but was only built in 1857. In London, the St Pancras Work-house Infirmary in Highgate opened in 1869, the large St Marylebone Workhouse Infirmary in 1881.

Nightingale faced some criticism regarding the pavilion model. For example, when, after a concerted campaign, she succeeded in getting a new Winchester Infirmary built at a new site, the pseudonymous Epicure de Grege Porcus wrote to the *Medical Times and Gazette* that the plans had been 'concocted' by Nightingale with 'an architect named [William] Butterfield, only known to me as a defacer of fine old churches and a builder of ugly new ones'.[2] He also pointed out that the new infirmary failed some of Nightingale's criteria: it was five storeys tall and, lying east–west, would have one set of windows facing north.

The long, narrow wards of the pavilion style, which became known as 'Nightingale wards', nevertheless soon became 'the dominant [hospital] accommodation in Britain, indeed very nearly the only available design for a nursing unit'. The design was excellent for ease of supervision as well as hygiene.[3] Patients liked it for, typically, the most serious cases were placed at the end closest to the ward sister, and were moved further away as they got better. The pavilions were spacious and airy, with privacy seldom an issue; a screen could be brought in between beds when needed. The need for the pavilion model diminished only when antibiotics became available and more patients could be treated and discharged, cured, after only a short stay.

Children's hospitals

Children's hospitals became popular beneficiaries of charitable giving in the nineteenth century. Nightingale, though, was always sceptical of their value. Since she had never nursed in a children's ward or children's hospital herself, she had to rely on observations from others. Good empiricist that she was, she wanted to see evidence of successful outcomes, and this was never collected.

The Lisbon Children's Hospital had in fact been the first hospital of any sort in whose establishment she was asked to assist; her friend Sidney Herbert made the approach, on behalf of the Prince Consort. The sad tale is that the King of Portugal had visited the English royal family with his new wife, a German princess, at Windsor Castle in 1858. Queen Stephanie died later that year, so that the hospital was to be a memorial to her. It still is, having been named in Portuguese the Hopital Dona Estefania. The plan, by a leading British architect, Albert Jenkins Humbert, is reproduced in Nightingale's *Notes on Hospitals*.

Twenty years after the building of the Lisbon Children's Hospital, Nightingale was asked by another member of the royal family, Princess Alice, by marriage the Grand Duchess of Baden, to consider plans for a new children's hospital in Heidelberg. Nightingale went to enormous trouble to find good examples, writing to doctors and nurses around the country, and reviewing and ruling out a number she obtained. She hoped that, by sending good sample plans to the princess, she and her allies would be asked to criticize their own plans, which indeed happened. Nightingale went over them herself and, following standard practice, received the comments of both Dr Sutherland and a Royal Engineer, Douglas Galton.

Nightingale took enormous care in her advice on children's wards to emphasize the need to prevent opportunities for neglect, cruelty or child abuse. Such terms, of course, were never used – however, what else could she have had in mind when stating that a children's ward 'demands publicity more than any part of the hospital', and explaining that children cannot complain? 'It should be the most frequented part of the hospital and nearest the superintendent,' she stated in the case of a children's ward designed to be placed on the top floor of the Montreal General.[4]

Nightingale is famous for her statement that no one should stay 'a day longer in hospital than is necessary for medical or surgical treatment'; for children, this was amended to 'not an hour longer'.[5] This meant having suitable convalescent care available outside the city, ideally at the seaside. Children were more vulnerable than adults to cross-infection. Children's hospitals also needed more staff than adult hospitals, almost a nurse per child, Nightingale thought. No child in hospital should be left alone, she said.

Nightingale's advice on hospital construction

During her life, Nightingale is known to have advised on the construction of at least 49 buildings, including convalescent hospitals and nurses' homes. The list of British hospitals on which she advised is impressive; they include institutions in Birkenhead, Blackburn, Buckinghamshire, Coventry, Derby, Devonport, Edinburgh, Glamorganshire, Glasgow, Leeds, Lincolnshire, Liverpool, London (several), Manchester, Netley, Norfolk, North Staffordshire, Oldham, Reading, Putney, Swansea, Winchester and Woolwich. Outside the UK, she advised on hospitals in Baltimore, Berlin, Carlsruhe, Heidelberg, Lisbon, Malta (three), Montreal, Moscow and Sydney, although for a number there is no surviving documentation.[6] (One can surmise that, beyond the fact that letters and old plans go missing, many architects did not keep the critical comments she sent them, which extended to 8 pages in the case of the Derby Infirmary, to 11 pages for the Women's Hospital, Euston Road and to a mere 7 for University College Hospital; meanwhile those for Johns Hopkins University Hospital extended to 12 pages.) Nightingale had an influence on the design of many more hospitals through her publications, without ever reviewing plans or corresponding with the architect or planners.

Being built of stone, many hospital buildings stood for well over a century, so that large numbers of unnecessary deaths could be brought about by mistakes in their design. Nightingale once remarked to her brother-in-law, who was inquiring about a hospital architect for a hospital in Buckinghamshire, 'I know no class of murderers who have killed so many people as hospital architects.'[7] Even St Thomas's Hospital, which became 'the most obvious, architecturally dramatic and best-known example of the new principles in use',[8] soon proved to have serious problems, with periodic outbreaks of infection that required the removal of patients and nurses. During an epidemic of diarrhoea and typhoid fever in 1885, 18 probationers had to be moved out. Nightingale exclaimed to Dr Sutherland: 'And Mr Currey is our architect! and Dr Bristowe is sanitary officer!!! to the hospital!!! I think I ought to be hanged and Dr Bristowe, Mr Currey, his builder and plumber shut up in a sink!!!'[9] She never forgot the consequences of bad hospital design.

6

Promoting health and better conditions in India

The Sepoy Mutiny, or First War of Indian Independence, broke out in the spring of 1857, less than a year after Nightingale's return from the Crimean War. On hearing of the lives lost, her instinct was to volunteer to go and nurse. Ill-health precluded that option, however, and in any event, Nightingale quickly came to realize that deaths from poor sanitation, suffered both by Indian nationals and soldiers, far outnumbered deaths from the mutiny.

The mutiny and its handling moved the British government to take over direct control of India. The Queen's Proclamation, read out in all Indian towns on 1 November 1858, ended 250 years of rule by the East India Company. After providing for the changeover in administration and the continuation of the rights of the rajahs and maharajahs, it boldly stated that Indians 'of whatever race or creed' had a right of appointment to all offices for which they were qualified 'by education, ability and integrity'. When Nightingale later wrote to the Queen about implementing this principle in a judicial matter, she praised it as a 'heaven-sent proclamation' and recalled how Indians greeted it 'with tears of hope and joy'. 'Like mercy,' she said, paraphrasing Portia in *The Merchant of Venice*, the proclamation 'becomes a monarch better than her crown'.[1]

In practice, however, discrimination was common. Furthermore, apart from the fact that educational qualifications meant English qualifications, all the most important decisions were made not in India but in London.

Nightingale's initial approach to India

Nightingale always aimed her reform efforts at what would make the most difference. China had a larger population than India, but was obviously not open to her. India was, and she had the ear of senior ministers who made major decisions on it. As soon as her Crimean War analysis was completed, therefore, she took up the matter of health and living conditions in the country, beginning what would become 40 years of research and advocacy. The task would bring her gradually into working relationships with major nationalists and social reformers.

Her partner at the outset was Sidney Herbert, who had chaired the Royal Commission on the Crimean War, and who now chaired a second one, on India. (He had to give up the role, for reasons of health, before it was finished, whereupon Nightingale chose as his replacement Lord Stanley.) She did much of the behind-the-scenes work on the India Royal Commission, as she had on that following the Crimean War. For India, she also prepared questionnaires for army stations and analysed the returns. The material produced led to the adoption of substantial reforms in barracks and hospitals, and in the amenities provided for soldiers. Progress on implementation was monitored by a further commission, set up after the Royal Commission on the Crimea, and whose major member was Dr Sutherland.

The Commission's official name shows its narrow mandate: the Royal Commission on the Sanitary State of the Army in India. Nightingale and her colleagues nonetheless broadened its terms by arguing that soldiers could not be kept healthy in stations where sanitary conditions in the surrounding areas were poor. She began with an attempt to carry out top-down reforms, conducting research to ascertain the problems, followed by carefully devised recommendations and a strategy for their implementation. She soon learned, however, that British officials had little incentive to act on even the most well-documented recommendations. Government, Cabinet, MPs, the press and voters were all answerable to British interests. The prevailing 'laissez-faire' political ethos held moreover that when, for example, famine loomed, intervention was thought only to make things worse – an excellent excuse, at least, for not acting.

Nightingale's first papers on India concern basic public health matters: sanitation, drainage and sewers. An early environmentalist, she understood the natural cycle between the decay of trees and their nourishment of the soil, and called for replanting of barren areas. She noted how canals helped the regrowth of forests in denuded terrain. She was aware that trees even helped to prevent cholera by improving drainage. She promoted the study of forestry, agriculture, botany and soils. When famine became the issue, she went on to consider its causes and prevention, examining land ownership, credit, rent, tenancy and gradually the need for local self-government. Some of her papers were delivered to progressive organizations, such as the Bengal Social Science Association (which made her an honorary member), the Poona Savajanik Sabha and the East India Association, as well as major British journals. Nightingale met with a steady stream of 'Indians', both Indian nationals and British officials in the Indian Service. The titles of these papers show the progression of her concerns:

'How People May Live and Not Die in India' (1863)
'On Indian Sanitation' (1870)
'Life or Death in India' (1873)
'Irrigation and Means of Transit in India' (1874, 1877)
'The Famine in Madras' and 'The Indian Famine' (1877)
'The United Empire and the Indian Peasant' (1878)
'A Water Arrival in India' (1878)
'The People of India' (1878)
'Irrigation and Water Transit' (1879)
'The Dumb Shall Speak and the Deaf Shall Hear' (1883)
'Our Indian Stewardship' (1883)
'To the Joint Secretaries of the Bombay Presidency Association' (1884)
Papers on Sanitation (1888, 1891, 1894)
'Village Sanitation in India' (1887 and 1894)
'Letter to the Public Health Society, Calcutta' (1888)
'Health Missioners for Rural India' (1896)

Nightingale's allies in India

Throughout her working life, Nightingale had superb allies: both progressive British officials and, increasingly, Indian nationals themselves, and sometimes their wives. Sir John (later Baron) Lawrence, the third Viceroy of India, was among the former; he began his term in January 1864, just when the recommendations of the Royal Commission needed implementation. Nightingale briefed him before his departure, and he wrote to her soon after his arrival to report on the first steps he had taken, the establishment of sanitary commissions in Calcutta, Madras and Bombay.[2] Other notable allies were the later Liberal viceroys Lord Ripon (1880–4) and Lord Dufferin (1884–8), the progressive governors of presidencies (as provinces were called, a hangover from rule by the East India Company), such as Sir Bartle Frere, Governor of Bombay, General Sir Arthur Cotton, Commandant of the Royal Engineers in Madras and an irrigation expert, and numerous sanitary officers of the presidencies and the government of India.

William Wedderburn (Fourth Baronet in 1882), Chief Secretary to the Bombay government, was a close friend and yet another ally. He edited *India: A Journal and Review of Indian Affairs*, started a high school in Pune and befriended numerous Indian nationals.

An ardent reformer, Wedderburn retired early in frustration; having returned to Scotland, he was an MP from 1893 to 1900, and became a leading opposition voice in Parliament on famine. In 1897, he moved for a full and independent inquiry into the condition of the masses. He noted that it was Queen Victoria's jubilee year – 50 years on the throne – yet one of terrible famine. Over four million people were on relief, and a tax on the poor was the means to supply the Famine Relief Fund. He opposed the war in South Africa, since wars always took money away from better causes, and thought it avoidable. Nightingale showed her appreciation of Wedderburn by bequeathing him a tidy £250 for 'an Indian object'.

In Parliament, Wedderburn and Dadabhai Naoroji were to form the Indian Parliamentary Committee, of which Wedderburn was the first chair. Naoroji (1825–1917) was a cotton trader, a Parsi who came to England in 1855 to start the first Indian company there. He became a supporter of Gopal Krishna Gokhale, mentor of Gandhi. When Gandhi arrived in England in 1888 to study law, one of the three letters of introduction he brought with him was to Naoroji, who by then was seeking to enter Parliament. (Gandhi himself had nothing but praise for Nightingale, and his own ceaseless promotion of sanitary measures perhaps owes something to her influence.)

Naoroji was the major founder of the East India Association, whose purpose was 'the independent and disinterested advocacy and promotion by all legitimate means of the public interests and welfare of the inhabitants generally'. With a number of wealthy Indians, including princes, providing the funding, the association – a predecessor of the Indian National Congress, of which Naoroji was also a co-founder – was launched in Bombay in 1865. Naoroji opened a London branch in 1866, and gave a lecture at its first public meeting in 1867. The association in England included retired officials who had returned home with enormous expertise and experience to offer, and were now unencumbered by the need to toe the government line. Women too, such as Mary Carpenter, took part in the meetings.

Naoroji's first lecture dealt with what would be a lifelong theme, the drain of resources from India to Britain, a process later to be termed 'underdevelopment'. Drain meant direct financial losses, as English officials (and businesses) sent their salaries and savings back to England, and spent their pensions there. There was also a 'moral drain' as the knowledge and experience they gained in India, whether in science, engineering or public administration, went back to England when they retired.[3] Naoroji's final volume on the subject, aptly titled *Poverty and UnBritish Rule in India*, came out in 1901.

The East India Association's meetings permitted reformers to develop their ideas from the perspective of the Indian population itself, at a time when all important decisions were made in the UK by Britons, and were enforced by British officials in India answerable to London. Parliamentary oversight was negligible; the House of Commons emptied when a member rose to speak on India. Nightingale was well aware of this. Papers read at the association's meetings were published in the *Journal of the East India Association* (1867 to 1941), and as pamphlets. Nightingale's paper of 1883 promises 'The Dumb Shall Speak and the Deaf Shall Hear'. In 1892, she wrote the introduction to a biography of the progressive Parsi journalist and social reformer Behramji Malabari.[4]

In 1883, the way was opened through the Ilbert Bill for Indian judges to hear European as well as Indian cases, as promised in the Queen's Proclamation of 1858; Europeans had previously been dealt with only by European judges. There was a terrific outcry in India, especially on the part of European wives. It was this that prompted Nightingale to write to the Queen, although her letter went unanswered; as well as stressing the great attachment Indians had to the terms of the proclamation, she raised local self-government and support for Indian industries as matters urgently needing action – Nightingale seldom kept to only one issue in her letters. Correspondence on India with her reform allies and her numerous papers take up two thick volumes in the *Collected Works of Florence Nightingale*.[5]

The politics of famine

Famines had been part of Indian life long before the British arrived. They grew more severe under British rule, however, as the growing of cash crops for export was favoured over the production of food for local consumption. Famines were a regional phenomenon, so that there were always some parts of the country with adequate harvests. To transport food from one area to another, however, required not only money, but the will to employ it for relief and adequate means of transport.

Relief moreover had to be timely, which was not the case in the Orissa famine of 1866, the first to occur after Nightingale took up the cause of India. Lord Salisbury, the new Secretary of State for India, had been warned, the day he took office, by a previous Governor General, Lord Ellenborough, of an impending 'terrible' famine. Ellenborough urged him to take measures in time, but Salisbury did nothing for two months. By the time he realized that outside help was needed, it was too late; the port of Orissa had been closed by the monsoons. A million people died as a result.[6]

Famine weakened people's resistance, so that probably more died from disease than from starvation itself; when Robert Rawlinson gave Nightingale an estimate that a million lives had been lost in the Crimean War, she noted that a million lives were lost 'every year from fever and epidemics in India'.[7] Famines were followed by inquiries and lengthy reports, but none of these led to serious change. Indeed, as happened during the potato famine in Ireland, food was still exported from districts in India that were suffering famine. Sir George Campbell, investigating the Orissa famine, called the rules for relief 'the most rigid', being informed by 'the driest political economy'. The board in question had 'the most unwavering faith in the "demand and supply theory"', so that they rejected with horror the importation of grain.[8]

The 'Great Famine' of 1876–8 occurred (again) under Conservative rule, as the government continued ruthlessly to observe laissez-faire principles. Food – a record 6.4 million hundredweight of wheat – continued to be exported to England, while the estimated death toll was 5.5 million. The total estimate of Indian deaths from famine under British rule in the second half of the nineteenth century is 29 million.[9]

Nightingale came to recognize that these were famines of both grain and money, the latter stemming from long-term desperate poverty. Landlords took so much of the peasants' produce that they could not save for bad times. When drought or floods occurred, they had no grain reserves and no money to purchase food or seed. Reform in land ownership, tenancy, rent and credit, as well as investment in infrastructure – canals, irrigation and railways – were essential to prevent famine.

Free-market 'liberalism' was essentially a Conservative philosophy, and the more radical Liberals gradually began to speak out against it. Nightingale hoped that Liberal governance of India, especially under Gladstone, a liberal on Ireland, would be better than that of the Conservatives. He proved not to be more liberal on India, but he was moved by the extreme meanness of the Conservatives on famine when in office from 1876 to 1880.

In the extraordinary election of 1880, Gladstone led the Liberal Party to a second victory (he was Prime Minister four times), running on foreign policy. He deliberately stood in the traditionally Conservative constituency of Midlothian, where vast crowds came to hear him deride Tory perfidy. In a speech delivered in St Andrew's Hall, Glasgow, he condemned the Conservatives' mismanagement as 'phantasmagoria . . . finance in confusion, legislation in intolerable arrear, honour compromised by the breach of public law, public distress aggravated by the destruction of confidence, Russia aggrandised and yet estranged, Turkey befriended but mutilated'. Africa was in a state of bloodshed, with a record 10,000 Zulus slain simply for defending their families, hearths and homes. He condemned the increased taxation imposed on the poorest Indians during the famine, one of the 'taxes on the poor' instituted being the infamous salt tax, contested by Gandhi decades later in a great 'Salt March'. There was nevertheless a 'deficiency of £6 million' in the money promised for a famine fund; Gladstone thundered: 'The money has been used. It is gone. It has been spent upon the ruinous, unjust, destructive war in Afghanistan.'[10] Nightingale called the campaign his 'Scottish jihad'.

It worked. Gladstone won a majority. As his Viceroy in India he appointed a known progressive, Lord Ripon, a former War Secretary and a friend of Nightingale's. Ripon was a Roman Catholic convert, a Christian socialist by philosophy, who had been influenced in his youth by F. D. Maurice, the leader of the Christian socialist movement. He was succeeded in 1884 by another close ally, Lord Dufferin – in fact Ripon magnanimously resigned early to permit another Liberal appointment before an expected change in government. (New governments made appointments from within their own party, but did not turn out someone already in place.)

Minor faults of the Conservative Viceroy Lord Lytton included his failure to provide irrigation information (regions with good irrigation were better able to avoid famine), and the institution of censorship with the Vernacular

Press Act. But Gladstone reserved his fiercest condemnation of the Conservatives for the extravagant durbar held in 1877 in Delhi to celebrate the Queen's acceptance of the title of Empress. This 'week-long feast for 68,000 officials, satraps and maharajahs' in a time of famine, he said, was 'the most colossal and expensive meal in world history'.[11]

Nightingale never went so far as Gladstone in blaming the Conservative government for the suffering of the Indian people, but she roundly condemned the diversion of Indian revenues for war in Afghanistan, and understood the consequential famine deaths. It was British policy to use Afghanistan as a buffer against Russia in order to protect its interests in India. Indian nationals, of course, gained nothing from the policy and had no say in it, yet they paid dearly for it in the diversion of resources needed for the relief and prevention of famine and for general economic development. After the death of Sir John Lawrence, Nightingale referred to his 'unerring knowledge and forecast' in opposing the Afghan war, glad that he had died before the 'appalling events' that had taken place at the Battle of Kabul.[12] She told the Undersecretary for India, Sir Louis Mallet, that people were so taken up by the war 'that they forget the far deeper tragedy', famine, taking place in southern India.[13]

Most viceroys of India came to visit Nightingale and exchanged correspondence with her. Lord Lytton was one of the few viceroys Nightingale never met. She later recalled that she had 'no communication at all' with him, although they had met when he was Colonial Secretary: 'I was very glad not to be employed by him.'[14]

7

Army reform and later wars

The UK government learned the painful lessons of the Crimean War well enough to avoid the many further wars that took place in the Balkans. Russia continued to expand, while the Ottoman Empire retracted. The UK also kept out of wars closer to home, such as the Austro-Prussian War of 1866 and the Franco-Prussian War of 1870–1, which gained Prussia Schleswig-Holstein and Alsace-Lorraine respectively. Britain would not go to war in Europe again until 1914. Instead, it used its forces to protect its considerable territory in India, its African colonies (with some expansion), and to manage its dominions in Canada, Australia and New Zealand.

The British Army – improving life for the ordinary soldier

Having advised on the formulation of the first Geneva Convention in 1864, Nightingale did a great deal of relief work, as did many British doctors, in the Franco-Prussian War. She also assisted with the relief of Bosnian and Bulgarian refugees during the Balkan Wars of 1875–9. Given her core mission to the sick poor, however, it is unsurprising that she should focus largely on the care and treatment of ordinary soldiers. Her belief that it was better to prevent illness than have to treat it later reinforced her determination to make the promotion of good health a priority, both for the army at home, in barracks and out on exercises, and on bases throughout the world.

In the course of conducting research for her post-Crimea reports, Nightingale had found out that the mortality rate in the army at home in peacetime was twice that of a similar male civilian age group. Given that soldiers had to be fit to be selected – the UK had no conscription at the time – their mortality rate should have been lower. Unhealthy living and working conditions were the likely culprits.

Such facts were laid out in the Royal Commission report, her own confidential report and her tribute to Sidney Herbert on his death, 'Army Sanitary Administration and its Reform under the late Lord Herbert'. Herbert himself chaired the four sub-commissions resulting from the Royal Commission, all of which were directed to improving the health of ordinary soldiers. Each sub-commission was charged with overseeing one of the following reforms:

1 Improved nutrition, with a cookery school located at the army base at Aldershot.
2 Reorganization of the Army Medical Department, both of hospital treatment services and a new 'sanitary service', for prevention. Nightingale noted that the army had regimental hospitals to care for the soldier 'in his *sickness*', but made 'no provision' for 'systematically caring for the soldier's *health*'.[1]
3 The creation of an Army Medical School, where the instruction was to include military 'hygiene', or preventive measures. Army doctors all had medical qualifications, but no training for the selection of sites for field hospitals and temporary quarters in the field.

4 Army medical statistics, to ensure the tracking of disease when it appeared, to catch epidemics early and to give timely feedback to the commanding officer of the state of the forces.

Further committees were established to make improvements in conditions such as the provision of 'day rooms', reading or coffee rooms, where soldiers could relax, chat, play board games and write home. These gave opportunities for recreation other than the tavern, and were well used.

Nightingale was a leader in this respect, and had the support of sometimes very senior officers. Despite the prevailing ethos that soldiers were 'brutes', she always considered the army to be an honourable profession, both for officers and men – it was joked that she saw them as 'Christian gentlemen'. For the men, however, much had to be done to make that life decent. Only a small percentage of soldiers were permitted to take a wife with them to a station; most, consequently, either could not marry, or had to leave their wife behind. Syphilis was a major disease, its victims at times occupying a third of army hospital beds. It could moreover be transmitted to the wife or partner and their offspring. The healthy occupations proposed by Nightingale helped to prevent recourse to prostitutes, and thereby the risk of contracting a sexually transmitted disease.

Nutrition for ordinary soldiers

The standard fare for soldiers in the British Army when Nightingale set to work on the matter was salt meat (beef or pork), hard biscuit (the French had baked bread), and a gill, or five ounces, of rum a day. Two distinct things had to be done to improve the men's diet. First was the adoption of regulations to make any new requirements obligatory, with specific requirements and sample menus for breakfast, lunch and dinner. Second, soldiers had to be trained to cook, hence the need to establish a cooking school. During the Crimean War, a start had been made on providing better food, thanks to the voluntary efforts of the French chef Alexis Soyer. As noted in Chapter 2, he showed how nutritious meals could be made, at no additional cost, by pooling rations. He introduced vegetables, preserved vegetables and rice, essential for preventing the scurvy endemic in the army during the Crimean War despite the fact that ways to prevent it had been discovered long before. However, much as everyone found Soyer's meals tasty when he gave a demonstration, soldiers could not produce the improved meals on their own. Concerted training was needed, as Nightingale understood.

The science of nutrition was young. Nightingale sought out the few known experts, including a civilian doctor, Robert Christison, and an army doctor, Thomas Alexander, later Director of the Army Medical Department, both trained in Edinburgh. Dr Sutherland advised on the nutritional value of preserved foods: 'We want for field service a dietary based on the nutritive power of preserved provisions, with the equivalent in nutritious value stated of fresh provisions (so much essence of beef equivalent to so much fresh beef or mutton).'[2] If the regulations were inadequate, Nightingale realized, decent food would not be produced, and the men's health would suffer.

The American Civil War

According to an American expert, noting their use by the Confederate Army of Virginia, Nightingale was responsible for 'the first known recommendations in modern literature for feeding military personnel'.[3] As happened during the Crimean War, 'more men died of disease caused by bad food and contaminated water (typhoid, dysentery and scarlet fever) than from all other battle losses.'[4] Her advice, published as *Directions for Cooking by Troops in Camp and Hospital*, 'prevented many losses from malnutrition and poor sanitation'.

Nightingale's advice on hospitals was followed by both sides in the Civil War. The Union Army had access to more of her material, which had been supplied by the author and abolitionist Harriet Martineau, though Nightingale thought they could have used it better – the American Civil War had an enormous death rate. The value of her Crimean War testimony was highlighted in a history of the United States Sanitary Commission, a voluntary organization that bore the same name as the official British commission.[5]

The Geneva Convention and the International Red Cross

Decent treatment of the wounded by the other side had begun long before the Geneva Convention, the Crimean War being but one example. The first Geneva Convention was nevertheless adopted in 1864 by a small number of countries; the UK added its signature at the next meeting. Its terms were initially limited to the protection of aid and relief workers assisting the wounded, although later provisions gave protection to prisoners of war and banned the use of weapons such as poison gases.

The War Office asked Nightingale in 1863 to prepare a briefing note for the British representative to the first meeting in Geneva. This was Dr William Rutherford, an old Crimean hand – an excellent surgeon, Nightingale acknowledged, but without knowledge of sanitary measures. Instructed only to observe and report back, he also did not know 'a blessed word of French', as he noted in his diary, where he described the new venture as 'a kind of international amateur society to assist the sick and wounded'. He agreed with Dr Sutherland and Nightingale, however, that 'each power should assist its own sick', and if they could not do that, 'they ought not to go to war at all.'[6]

In response to the Geneva Convention, Red Cross (later Cross and Crescent) societies came into existence in many countries. The founder of the Red Cross movement, the Swiss businessman Henri Dunant, had been motivated by seeing the wounded of both sides left on the field at Solferino, in the Italian war of independence of 1859, and he cited Nightingale as being his inspiration. Nightingale herself was always sceptical, fearful that letting governments off caring for their own sick and wounded – by expecting volunteers to do it – would make war 'cheap'. Indeed, her fears were realized: by ennobling sacrifice, aid societies helped to give war an air of legitimacy. Dunant himself became disillusioned, embracing pacifism at the end of his life.

A much later analysis was to credit Nightingale with being 'correct in her prediction that the existence of Red Cross societies would "render war more easy"'. By the late nineteenth century, armies were using the Red Cross 'to efficiently recycle wounded men back into the front lines'.[7] An English voluntary aid worker reported to Nightingale that the Prussians were selling the society's stores at Amiens at a tenth of their cost.[8]

The Franco-Prussian War

Prussia's aggression in the Austro-Prussian War over Schleswig-Holstein, in 1866, can be seen as the first step towards the two world wars of the twentieth century. Prussia's success led to the formation of the North German Confederation, the core of Prussia, in August of that year, with Wilhelm I as Emperor/Kaiser and Otto von Bismarck as Chancellor. In 1870, Bismarck provoked Napoleon III into declaring war on Prussia; France lost, at a terrible cost, and Napoleon went into exile in England. Nightingale called the conflict 'this most terrible of all earth's wars'.[9]

While Britain stayed out of these wars, its National Aid Society, forerunner of the British Red Cross, sent doctors, supplies and 'ambulances', or field hospitals. Nurses were not required – both the French and Germans had nuns, the Germans deaconesses. But Nightingale assisted behind the scenes in getting supplies to the right place, insisting on giving both sides equal treatment; both awarded her a medal for her help.

The Crown Princess of Prussia was Britain's Princess Royal, eldest daughter of Queen Victoria, a friend of Nightingale and an avid promoter of reformed nursing. Nightingale's sympathies were nevertheless with France, and she was torn by the terrible siege of Paris, in which many starved. She helped raise funds for relief both in the city and for ruined farmers.

Later wars: Afghanistan, Anglo-Zulu, Transvaal and Egypt

Nightingale played no role in the Second Afghan War of 1878, but she deplored its terrible consequences for India. She later noted that Salisbury and Lytton, the Conservative Prime Minister and Viceroy, 'made' the Afghan War, while Gladstone and Granville, the Liberal Prime Minister and Foreign Secretary, made the Sudan War.

The Anglo-Zulu War of 1879 resulted in an expansion of the British Empire in southern Africa. In response, during this 'hideous' war, Nightingale asked an Indian administrator rhetorically about the prospect of administering the Transvaal and Zululand: 'besides Natal and what more! *have* we succeeded so well in India that we want South Africa too?'[10] The conflict was followed by the Transvaal War, or First Boer War, of 1880–1. Nightingale was involved not only in sending nurses to the latter conflict but – yet again – in calling for an investigation of defects in the hospitals. She had a number of women allies now, who reported problems to her and joined her in pressing for changes. Amy Hawthorn, wife of a colonel and cousin of General Gordon, told her of the 'painful' defects in hospitals set up at the British base Fort Amiel. Nightingale remarked that, 27 years later, it was Crimea 'all over again', albeit on a smaller scale.[11]

The first Egyptian campaign followed soon after the Transvaal War, in 1882. Egypt was strategically important to Britain on account of the Suez Canal, which made for its shortest route to India. The country was controlled by Britain and France, who provided revenues to its ruler, the Khedive, to run a flagrantly corrupt government. From 1875, Britain held a majority of shares in the Suez Canal

Company. However, a nationalist uprising in 1882 threatened to upset these cosy arrangements. Britain sent an expeditionary force under General Garnet Wolseley, while British and French naval forces bombarded Alexandria – without a declaration of war, as Nightingale noted.[12] The expeditionary force arrived on 20 May 1882 and, after being stopped in its first attempt to march on Cairo, used the Suez Canal to approach the city. It won a decisive battle at Tel-el-Kebir, north of Cairo, on 12 September.

By now, in contrast with the days of the Crimea, trained nurses were available, some with army experience, and Nightingale duly organized their dispatch. General Wolseley told her that they would be in and out fast, and this proved to be the case, although some had to be sent back to deal with ongoing illness among the troops. The nurses were based at Cairo and in Lower Egypt, with some stationed on a hospital ship off Suakim. Nightingale received regular reports, both from the medical staff and from an agent of the National Aid Society.

A cholera epidemic, which broke out in Egypt in 1883, greatly increased the workload. Doctors and nurses alike were forced to extend their stay, and a research team was sent out to investigate the causes of the disease. Nightingale's comments on Egypt are informed by her travels there in 1849–50, when she visited pyramids and ruins, and took a lengthy boat ride along the Nile. She regarded Cairo as spectacularly beautiful.

The purpose of the second Egyptian campaign, in 1885, was the rescue of General Gordon and his forces, who were being held captive in Khartoum. Sudan at the time was under the control of Egypt, which itself was now in the hands of the British. The crisis was caused by a rebel leader, the Mahdi, who had a divine mission to purify Islam from the European governments that defiled it. General Gordon, a former Governor General of Sudan, was sent to Khartoum ostensibly to evacuate it. Instead, he stayed, bringing in some reforms (for example destroying instruments of torture), but also accommodating slave traders. The Mahdists in 1884 surrounded Khartoum and held it siege for eight months.

Gladstone was slow in sending relief. No longer the 'GOM' – 'grand old man' – he gained the new nickname of 'MOG', 'murderer of Gordon', when the expeditionary force arrived too late. How Gordon died is not known, but his head was presented to the Mahdi on a spear. Nightingale, as it happened, knew Gordon personally. She respected his faith, but did not support his violation of the terms of his mission.

Part 2

THE LEGACY

8

Nursing: the profession of patient care

The prime means of establishing the nursing profession throughout the world was the Nightingale School of Nursing. The nurses it trained took new methods and higher standards first to other hospitals in the United Kingdom, and then to hospitals in many other countries. The Edinburgh Royal Infirmary, which gained a team in 1872, became in effect another 'Nightingale School', sending out matrons and nurses across Scotland. Belfast and then Dublin were early in getting professional nursing started, Oxford and Cambridge relatively late. Nightingale had a direct hand in establishing nursing in many northern and Midland cities, including Liverpool, Birmingham, Derby, Leeds, Lincoln and Wolverhampton.[1]

A team of matrons and nurses went out to Sydney, Australia, in 1868, and another to Montreal in 1875; the latter, however, soon came back, so that professional nursing was not established in Canada until much later. In the United States, three nursing schools on the Nightingale model opened, although without nurses from her school, in the early 1870s. Nightingale met and mentored the first trained American nurse, Linda Richards, in 1877. Richards started professional nursing in numerous American hospitals, then took it as a missionary to Japan.

Many countries got their start in nursing by sending women to London for experience, although they did not undergo the full training programme. Nightingale usually met them, and she kept in touch with some of them for years. There are examples from Prussia, Baden, Hesse-Darmstadt and Sweden, as well as some from the United States and Canada. Roman Catholic countries with nursing orders were much later to establish training schools. The impetus in France came from a woman doctor, Anna Hamilton, and first met with success in Bordeaux, the most Protestant (Huguenot) region of France. In Italy, the breakthrough came when secular English and American women sought out Italians who would work with them to establish a training school. In Ireland, religious orders did not establish training schools until the 1890s, so that Nightingale nursing was limited to hospitals with some Protestant leadership.[2]

Nursing to a professional level in army hospitals followed that in civilian institutions. It was impossible to provide army hospitals with nursing schools of their own; in peacetime, they lacked the serious cases needed for training purposes, while in war the pressure was too great for experienced nurses to be sidelined into training. The answer was to provide regular training at a civil hospital – initially at St Thomas's – to be followed by working experience at an army hospital. At first this took place at the army hospital at Netley, near Southampton, and then, when it opened, at the Herbert Hospital in Woolwich. By the time of the Egyptian campaigns of 1882 and 1885, almost 30 years after Crimea, numerous suitably trained nurses were available to send.

There was too little space to accommodate the teaching of home nursing, or 'district nursing', which began roughly a decade after Nightingale's nursing school opened. It required regular hospital training, followed by supervised experience by qualified district nurses.

Nightingale's final initiative in health promotion was a project to introduce 'health visitors' – 'missioners', as she called them. Strictly speaking these were not nurses. The scheme was developed with the Buckinghamshire Medical Officer of Health, Dr George H. De'ath, and actively supported by Frederick Verney and the North Bucks Technical Education Committee. The visitors, all 'ladies', or educated women, were given a series of lectures by the medical officer, before taking a formal examination set and marked by a committee of public health doctors. A certificate was awarded to those who passed.

The visitors were then sent to visit mothers in rural areas. That the programme was a success can be judged by the positive reception of the visits, and the fact that other counties followed suit. Nightingale's own doctor told her that earlier such attempts had failed.

In her short paper on the project, she argued for a cooperative relationship between local government and the people, as opposed to a coercive one. Not the least reason for the health visitors programme was that 'It is much cheaper to promote health than to maintain people in sickness.'[3]

Nightingale's contribution to nursing in all its modes can hardly be overstated. She led the profession until her retirement. Even in her later years she kept up with medical developments that affected nursing, such as operating theatre procedures. She continued to resist the 'preliminary training' of nurses, in other words having them start with academic work rather than on the wards. Some Nightingale nurses, such as Rebecca Strong at the Glasgow Royal Infirmary, nevertheless made the move. Isabel Hampton, matron at Johns Hopkins University Hospital, not only made its training programme more academic, she herself gave lectures, not a practice Nightingale ever contemplated. Hampton then used the material when writing her important nursing textbook, *Nursing: Its Principles and Practice*, one of the first by a nurse to surpass Nightingale's early *Notes on Nursing*.

Another Nightingale nurse, A. L. Pringle, who as Matron at Edinburgh and St Thomas's had never allowed preliminary training, praised it in her 1905 nursing book.[4] Such an approach, however, was not introduced to the Nightingale School until after its founder's death, although she had no role in decision-making, nor even met with the matron, after 1898.

Improving the status of nurses

Nightingale had always wanted army nurses, like doctors, to be treated as officers. Before her time, the few 'nurses' employed by the army had the status of private, reported to a sergeant and earned less than a laundress or cook.[5] Officer status for nurses was achieved only late in the nineteenth century.

The career of Louisa Parsons, who began her training at the Nightingale School in 1879, exemplifies this development. She served in both the Egyptian Campaign of 1882, which put her on the first awards list for a Royal Red Cross, and that of 1885. Parsons subsequently moved to the United States, where she served as Assistant Matron at Johns Hopkins and in 1889 was appointed Matron at the University of Maryland Hospital, both in Baltimore. She nursed for the US Army in the Spanish–American War of

1898, and again for the British in the Boer War. When she died, in Oxford in 1916, she was given the full honours of a military funeral. The ceremony was described by Lady Osler, wife of Sir William Osler, Regius Professor of Medicine at Oxford, who had known Parsons in Baltimore and attended the funeral: 'The coffin was carried to the church on a gun carriage – a company of soldiers, buglers and a firing party – rifles fired over the grave and the "Last Post" called by the buglers.' It was an 'immensely impressive' ceremony, the street lined with people from far and near.[6]

The low status of nurses when Nightingale's school opened in 1860 is indicated by their classification in the 'Domestic Service' category of the UK Census. By 1881, they had been promoted to 'Subordinate Medical Service' and in 1891 were given their own category as 'Sick Nurse, Midwife or Invalid Attendant', leaving 'Nursemaids' and 'Children's Nurses' in the domestic category.[7] There was a parallel elevation in status in job descriptions in the United States Census.

Nursing eventually became a major occupation for women throughout the world. By 2009 the World Health Organization estimated that there were nearly 20 million nurses in total; they numbered 6,620,000 in Europe (including some 621,000 in the UK), 2,927,000 in the USA, 1,431,000 in India, 350,000 in Canada and 201,000 in Australia.[8]

Nightingale's influence, albeit indirect, can be seen as late as the mid-twentieth century, when professional nursing developed in Africa. The leader of the nursing profession in Nigeria, Kofoworola Abeni Pratt (c. 1910–93), trained as a Nightingale nurse, was supported by the Nightingale Fund for further work and was inspired by Nightingale. She was probably the first black nurse to work in the National Health Service. When she returned to Nigeria she successfully contended with the racist practices of senior expatriate administrators, becoming the first Nigerian Chief Nurse in her country, and led the way in promoting Nigerians to senior positions in the country's nursing and medical services.

Hospital responsibility for working conditions

Nurses, Nightingale always held, were in hospitals for 'the care of the sick', which was 'the real purpose of their being there at all'. As she argued in 'Method of Improving the Nursing Service of Hospitals' (1867), they were not 'to act as lifts, water carriers, beasts of burden, or steam engines – articles whose labour can be had at vastly less cost than that of educated human beings'.

As employers, hospitals had responsibilities for their employees' health and safety. Nightingale was well aware that doctors and nurses, like their patients, could die as a result of insanitary conditions. In 'Method of Improving the Nursing Service of Hospitals', she also stated:

> Every employer of labour is bound to provide for the health of the workers. And any society which professes to provide for sick, and so provides for them that the lives of nurses and of medical officers have to be sacrificed in the discharge of their duties, gives sufficient proof that providing for the care of sick is not its calling.

Furthermore, she noted, 'As it happens, the arrangements required for the welfare of sick are the very same which are required for the health of nurses.' Again she specified that nurses were there for their 'constant attendance on sick', meaning that their role was not to do the hospitals' cleaning.[9] Her insistence on hospitals' responsibilities as employers for their employees' health and safety is part of her legacy, a subject it seems that no one else broached at the time; and her advice is perhaps as necessary today as it was when she wrote it, some 150 years ago.

The rise in nursing expertise

As medical science developed, so did nursing. Nightingale's own writings show this, her articles of the 1880s and early 1890s dealing with the vast increase in tasks to be mastered. While mere handwashing with soap had been promoted in 1860, there were now specific types and strengths of disinfectants for different procedures. As aseptic practices came into use, the instructions became still more complex. While nurses were not initially allowed to take a patient's temperature, moreover, they would later be assigned urine tests, subcutaneous injections and the fitting of catheters. All this became possible as compulsory state education ensured that nurses had a much higher level of education than in Nightingale's early years.

The modern development of the nurse practitioner is a logical evolution of the Nightingale model. The doctor still diagnoses and determines treatment, but the nurse practitioner has much more discretion in carrying out instructions, and is authorized to make many decisions on her or his own. The participation of nurses in policy development teams also fits Nightingale's vision for nursing, although again she never foresaw such a development occurring in the near future.

Indeed, as the profession evolved, it became increasingly attractive to men, a development entirely consistent with Nightingale's views, though not one she ever forecast. When she began her work, women were neither allowed in medicine nor in any other profession. Now they are, and in some countries they are numerically dominant in medicine. Women today are excluded from few occupations – although the bearded Greek Orthodox priest springs to mind as one such. Nightingale's concern for women's jobs and income was always secondary to the goal of providing skilled patient care, but the establishment of nursing as a decent career for women was among her goals from the beginning. She never considered that men were incapable of becoming good nurses, however, and fully expected that most military nursing would be done by men. For them, as for women nurses, she urged better training and working conditions.

Nightingale gave encouragement to the medical doctors who promoted preventive medicine in the late nineteenth century, and they quoted her writings in pursuing this work. Her friend Sir Henry Acland was a leading member of the British Medical Association Committee on State Medicine, a major means of making the case for stronger laws and regulations on health. Her insistence on the influence of environmental factors in the promotion or otherwise of health demanded careful attention to the biophysical environment. Prevention was better than cure, but required knowledge of complex causal factors and special training to that end.

A late example is 'Health and Local Government' (1894), when she cited the lives lost, the weakened health of survivors and doctors' bills as the cost of neglect. Although she occasionally indulged in hyperbole, once claiming that 'Preventable disease should be looked upon as social crime',[10] the importance of prevention can be seen in her work from beginning to end.

9

The National Health Service

Nightingale never anticipated a large, national, public health service such as was legislated in the UK in 1946 by the post-war Labour government. Nothing close to it could have been brought into being, however, without the massive improvements, both in hospital design and nursing care, achieved in the late nineteenth century, and which she so effectively promoted. As noted in Chapter 4, most people who had to enter a hospital in the nineteenth century had no recourse but to substandard institutions that gave no nursing care and relied on bed sharing. Although Nightingale never envisaged a comprehensive public system, she was always pragmatic. What works? At what price? Single-payer systems save enormously on costs – administrative and legal – and produce better results, as shown in such indicators as life expectancy and childhood deaths.

The great barrier in the UK to a decent hospital system for all, for so many years, was the principle of the Poor Law, known as 'less eligibility', which meant its provision must be less than what someone could earn at the worst-paid job. This effectively excluded those affected from access to quality medical and nursing care. Louisa Twining challenged this early on, calling for a separate administration of Poor Law hospitals to be supported by taxes. Nightingale subsequently, as the social administration expert Brian Abel-Smith has pointed out, devised 'the administrative structure within which the plan could have been put into immediate operation'. He notes the irony that 'eighty years later, what had been the philosophy of a few pioneer women of the upper class became the rationale of the National Health Service Act' introduced by a Labour government.[1]

Under Nightingale's influence, new buildings, some using the model pavilion design (see p. 40), were added to the old workhouse infirmaries. Some infirmaries not only hired trained nurses, after the Nightingale School gave them a start, but established training schools of their own. As a result, when the National Health Service came into operation in 1948, there was no need to construct new buildings. The preceding decades had raised standards to a reasonable level. The old civilian hospitals, under their own voluntary boards, the workhouse infirmaries, under their parish boards of guardians, and the new publicly funded fever hospitals and asylums were all nationalized to form the new hospital system.

The famous Edith Cavell, who was executed in 1915 by the Germans for assisting the escape of British and Belgian soldiers, was among those who nursed in both the regular and workhouse system in England before taking a civil nursing post in Belgium. After training at the London Hospital, the largest civil hospital in the UK, she nursed at Shoreditch Workhouse Infirmary before becoming first night nurse, then night superintendent, at the St Pancras Workhouse Infirmary.

The first workhouse infirmary to get a model building – Chorlton, near Manchester – was not Nightingale's responsibility, but many that followed were the result of her pressure – and of her bribes, in that a workhouse would be given trained Nightingale nurses if it opted for a new, improved building. The St Pancras Workhouse Infirmary, relocated to Highgate and known thereafter as the Highgate Infirmary, was the first of these. Nightingale was sufficiently pleased with the plans that she agreed to send nurses there to introduce professional nursing. The St Marylebone Workhouse Infirmary was a later example. Its new building, designed by the leading architect Henry Saxon Snell, was opened by the Prince and Princess of Wales; its new nurses' home, built a little later, was opened by Princess Christian.

The changing names of such institutions show the progress made. The St Marylebone Workhouse Infirmary became the St Marylebone Hospital in 1923; then, when it was taken over by the London County Council in 1930, it was renamed St Charles Hospital. The Chorlton Union Workhouse Infirmary became Withington Hospital, and was later to become part of University Hospitals of South Manchester. Shoreditch Workhouse Infirmary was renamed St Leonard's Hospital in 1920.

Universal health coverage

The NHS became an international model when it was launched in 1948, because it provided 'what no other country in the world has achieved at the same cost: universal health care in the form of equal access to comprehensive care, irrespective of personal income'.[2] Canada's public healthcare system was greatly influenced by the NHS, and has common roots with it in the Christian response to the story of the Good Samaritan in the Gospels. Canada's great founder of public healthcare, T. C. Douglas, was a Baptist minister in the Christian socialist tradition. He had himself needed expensive medical care as a child, which would have been unavailable to him but for the charity of a doctor. The country's medicare system was first introduced in the province of Saskatchewan, when Douglas was premier in what was the first Labour-type government in North America. NHS doctors had to be recruited to Saskatchewan when local doctors went on strike against the introduction of public medicare – which they had previously agreed to, before succumbing to a massive campaign by the American Medical Association.

National healthcare in Canada was legislated under a minority Liberal government in 1965, with support from Douglas's party; Lester Pearson, the Liberal Prime Minister, was himself the son of a Methodist minister. The politics were a variation of those in the UK, when a Labour government legislated to establish the National Health Service proposed by a commission whose head was a Liberal, William Beveridge.

The United States remains an exception to world trends, as the only developed nation not to have a public healthcare system. Obamacare, or the Affordable Care Act of 2010, brought health *insurance* to millions more Americans, but fell short of being a full single-payer, taxpayer-financed, system. It, in turn, became the target of Donald Trump on his election as president in 2016. An estimated 45,000 Americans died in 2009 from lack of health coverage. Deaths attributable to lack of coverage exceeded those from kidney disease.[3]

The purpose of the NHS has been watered down since its founding – although more in England than in Scotland or Wales – as have similar provisions in other prosperous countries. Privatization, the market allocation of services and fees or co-payments for certain services are now the rule in England under the Health and Social Care Act 2012.

This act was legislated under a coalition Conservative–Liberal Democrat government, elected in 2010, which had no such mandate but rather had promised to end 'top-down' changes in the NHS. Critics deplore the fundamental change in philosophy occasioned by the removal of the 'duty to care' of the original act. They reject the excuse of lack of resources as a justification and note that costs in real terms declined in 2011–12 compared with 2009–10, and that Scotland and Wales can still afford care for all. It is telling that the campaign to reinstate the 'duty to care' has been led by Lord Owen, a Liberal Democrat peer, formerly a Labour Minister of Health, the same Liberal–Labour combination that instituted the NHS in the first place. How this will play out is not clear.

But how do these changes in the NHS relate to Nightingale's principles of care? Obviously Nightingale anticipated neither the NHS as a provider of services, nor its dilution after 60 years of successful operation. The new law abandons the core principle of quality care for all, regardless of ability to pay. The commercialization of hospitals was never a consideration in the nineteenth century, when hospitals were either voluntary, non-profit – the civil hospitals – or public, in the case of military and Poor Law hospitals. Hospitals for profit? Nursing conglomerates bidding for contracts? Cleaning services contracted out to save money? All this would be news to her, although the changes would need to be judged on the basis of their results.

While high-income countries with good public health-care systems have gradually accepted some measure of privatization, for countries where incomes are lower the challenge is still to provide quality care to all. The World Health Organization (WHO) calls this 'Universal health coverage', and sees public measures as key, without forbidding any particular private measure. The WHO asserts in its constitution 'the highest attainable standard of health as a fundamental right of every human being'. The words 'appropriate' and 'affordable' qualify this right, and public provision is not a requirement. 'Universal health coverage' is said to be 'a means to promote the right to health', but is evidently not the only means. Furthermore, just as Nightingale explained that people lost everything in her day by having to pay medical and hospital bills, so that whole families had to enter the workhouse, the WHO today notes that 'about 100 million people a year' are pushed below the poverty line on account of healthcare expenditure.[4]

When the United Nations, in 2000, selected its 'millennium goals' for 2015, health was third on the list, after poverty and hunger, before illiteracy, environmental degradation and discrimination against women. We will return to the concept of health as a right in the next chapter, along with the related issue of the welfare state.

10

Mainstream social and political reform

As a lifelong Liberal, Nightingale was consistent in her political views at a time of considerable flux. The name Karl Marx appears nowhere in her writing; nor do the words communism or socialism. Yet Nightingale was as opposed as Marx to the laissez-faire liberalism prevalent in their day. She condemned the misery produced by unrestrained capitalism in overcrowding and squalid conditions, malnutrition and disease, as she did the starvation that was the lot of millions in India under Britain's laissez-faire administration.

The great difference between Nightingale and Marx is that she thought that capitalism could be reformed, while he saw its overthrow, with the abolition of private ownership of the means of production and distribution, as the only solution. Nightingale not only rejected revolution as dangerous, she believed that systemic change could be achieved by legislation, and she was able to prove as much. Furthermore, she thought such large-scale changes should be brought in gradually, to ensure that the intended reforms actually worked. Healthcare and living conditions did improve in Britain in the second half of the nineteenth century; the gap between rich and poor actually declined.

The status of women

Thanks largely to Nightingale, nursing became the first profession in Britain open to women, in an era when women wishing to teach were effectively limited to taking dependent situations as governesses in families. Nursing for a time was the highest-paid profession for women in Britain.

Nightingale played a more peripheral role in promoting other reforms for women: suffrage, married women's property rights and access to university education and civil service jobs. All these were given her attention, sometimes her dues or a donation, but minimal time commitment. She was, however, the first opponent of the discriminatory Contagious Diseases Acts, which targeted women prostitutes, rather than men, in the attempt to reduce syphilis in the army and navy. Josephine Butler led the final campaign, while Nightingale helped from the sidelines.[1]

Women did not get the vote nationally in the UK until 1918, when it was granted to those aged 30 and over. The struggle for suffrage can be identified as dating from 1866, when John Stuart Mill presented to Parliament a petition – of which Nightingale was a signatory – demanding equal political rights for women. Nightingale would sign further petitions or letters in favour of the vote in 1872, 1873, 1874, 1875 and 1878. She also signed petitions proposing married women's property legislation in 1869, university admission in 1875 and education for women in India in 1892; she told her sister, in fact, that she signed about 20 petitions every year.[2]

Women first entered university education in Britain, in small numbers, in the late nineteenth century. London University admitted its first women in 1878, and Nightingale was one of those to sign an 'address of thanks'.[3] She encouraged and gave practical assistance to leaders of women's higher education such as Anne Jemima Clough, the first Principal of Newnham College, Cambridge. At Clough's request, Nightingale reviewed the plans for the college and found them 'as bad as they possibly can be . . . in almost every respect', as she told Dr John Sutherland when she asked him to add his comments to her eight pages.[4]

In 1874, Nightingale mentored the first woman to hold a professional position in the public service in England. This was Jane Senior, Poor Law inspector and daughter-in-law of the economist Nassau Senior. Nightingale not only gave her moral support, but composed a questionnaire for her on Poor Law institutions. Nightingale later met with and encouraged Umeko Tsuda, a Japanese pioneer in women's education. She encouraged the provision of women doctors to India and education for Indian women.

The making of the welfare state

In addition to her campaigns for the reform of workhouse infirmaries, Nightingale supported the virtual abolition of the Poor Law itself. Workhouse relief was deliberately punitive, intended to deter people from seeking help. Nightingale understood, however, that the vast majority of inmates, possibly over 90 per cent, were incapable of work on account of old age, illness, disability or chronic infirmity, while children should never be in a workhouse at all. She sought care facilities suited to their needs, quality hospital care for the sick to get them out again.

Nightingale was disappointed with the Metropolitan Poor Law Act, adopted in 1867 under a Conservative government. Yet Brian Abel-Smith would later call it 'an important step in English social history', no less than the 'first explicit acknowledgement that it was the duty of the state to provide hospitals for the poor'.[5] Nightingale influenced the Poor Law inspector H. B. Farnall, who wrote the report that led to the bill; the similarity in style, Abel-Smith remarks, 'suggests that large sections of it were written by Miss Nightingale herself'.[6] Another reforming step was made in 1929 with the passage of the Local Government Act, which transferred control of Poor Law hospitals from their boards of guardians to counties and county boroughs, a change recommended by Nightingale 65 years earlier.[7]

Nightingale not only had a better understanding of the numbers and types of cases in the workhouse system than virtually everyone else, she had a thoroughly distinct approach, informed by her faith. As she told Edwin Chadwick, himself a Poor Law expert, the sick 'man, woman or child' was not a pauper to be 'repressed', but 'a fellow creature to be nursed into health'. The care of the sick poor, 'and indeed of all persons labouring under physical or mental disability to win their bread, is a thing totally different from the government of paupers'.[8]

Nightingale understood the stigma entailed in going into a workhouse infirmary, although she did not use the term. To avoid it, infirmaries not only needed quality buildings, medical and nursing care, but they had to be seen to be distinct from the old workhouses, hence her recommendation that they should be administered separately. Her 'ABC' of reform set this out:

the separation of the sick, insane, infirm and aged, incurable, imbecile and children;

the creation of a single, central administration;

to place all those 'suffering from disease, bodily or mental' into a distinct system responsible to Parliament.[9]

As noted in Chapter 4, the legislation adopted only *permitted* the hiring of trained nurses, but did not *require* it. Thus reforms had to be won piecemeal, typically when the reform-minded president of a board of guardians gave leadership. In fact, many workhouse infirmaries were brought up to a decent standard in the late nineteenth century. In the twentieth century, their amalgamation with regular civil hospitals helped to diminish the stigma, a process aided in some cases by a change in name.

Not until the Royal Commission on the Poor Law of 1909 were reforms on the scale advocated by Nightingale again contemplated. Substantial changes were not adopted even then, but an influential minority report, written by such notable reformers as Sidney and Beatrice Webb, gained them wide circulation. Many reforms were brought in by a Liberal government with support from Labour MPs, elected for the first time in 1906: school meals in the same year, old-age pensions for persons 70 and older in 1908, labour exchanges in 1909, and national insurance for the employed in 1911.

Nightingale had been an advocate of labour exchanges as early as 1869, when she explained in 'A Note on Pauperism' that 'the faculty of finding work is quite a peculiar one', and the 'great mass of workmen' were not capable, when work failed them, of finding it elsewhere.[10] Indeed, her views on labour exchanges reflect her discussions with working men even before Crimea. The rules for obtaining local relief, moreover, discouraged the unemployed from looking elsewhere. Instead of telling people to go into the work-house, Nightingale believed, the authorities should say, 'Come and we will help you to find work.' People needed 'training' in obtaining work, she added. Economic 'doctrine' held that supply and demand regulated the price of everything, labour included, but there was no way for supply to find demand. Nightingale did not use the term 'Christian socialism' in her 'Pauperism' paper, but her ideas reflect and promote its ideas, which were then beginning to gain considerable support.

Nightingale expected the private sector to run the economy normally, but in times of severe distress, as in Spitalfields in 1860 and Sheffield in 1864, public intervention was needed. In a letter to her Liberal MP brother-in-law she asked: 'Is it possible to believe that the state could not give (at least in times of exceptional distress) productive work at remunerative prices?' She did not want made work or charity.[11] Detailed justification for such intervention would not appear until the Great Depression, with John Maynard Keynes's *General Theory of Employment, Interest and Money* (1936).

What influence Nightingale might have had on these later developments is not clear. Certainly her bold ideas reached some leading political figures, including a Liberal President of the Poor Law Board, C. P. Villiers, John Stuart Mill, then a radical MP, and Edwin Chadwick. The Beveridge Report of 1942 would articulate more broadly the philosophy of the welfare state, with comprehensive recommendations on each of the five 'giant evils' to be overcome: want, disease, squalor, ignorance and idleness, good strong words all.[12] The massive mobilization of the war years made such fundamental change seem practicable, and the sacrifices made for the war provided justification. The post-war Labour government was prompt in bringing in a Family Allowances Act in 1945, and the National Insurance Act and National Health Act in 1946. The National Assistance Act in 1948 both brought in new measures and abolished the old Poor Law itself, declaring in Section 1: 'The existing poor law shall cease to have effect.' Nightingale had condemned it as early as 1866.

From a situation in which the state, at the parish level, provided only minimal relief to the destitute, now the prevention of poverty itself became the goal of the national state. Knowledge, grounded in adequate statistics, could lay out the dimensions of need and guide the implementation of solutions. This was all very much in line with Nightingale's approach.

The political constellation that achieved this transformation is worth noting. Like Nightingale herself, William Beveridge, an economist, was a Liberal, and he later became Liberal leader in the House of Lords. Before the war, he had been director of the London School of Economics, a creation of socialists such as Sidney and Beatrice Webb and George Bernard Shaw. He had served in Winston Churchill's wartime government, in which the Labour leader Clement Attlee was Deputy Prime Minister. When the Conservatives regained power in 1951, with Churchill returning as Prime Minister, the welfare state provisions remained in place. Churchill himself had started his political life as a Liberal.

Nightingale never used 'rights' language in arguing for better measures against the existing Poor Law, but such language is the current currency. Rights can be seen to have evolved naturally from the principles of the late eighteenth-century Enlightenment. Nightingale, by contrast, used faith-based arguments: the tie to our fellow creatures, under God. This concept of a bond, through sympathy or compassion, also has strong Enlightenment roots, both religious, in the moral philosophy school, and secular, in utilitarianism. The secular Adam Smith, who was probably an agnostic (there is not even an RIP on his tombstone), nonetheless gave a pivotal role to 'sympathy' in his *Theory of Moral Sentiments* (1759). Nightingale asserted that 'the same tie really connects us to every one of our fellows as the tie which connects us with God'. This meant that 'to neglect or ill use the imbecile old woman, the dirty child, is the same crime of *lèse majesté* against the Almighty that blasphemy of God is.'[13]

India: from reform to independence

Significant reform in India did not happen in Nightingale's lifetime, but steps were taken that would eventually, in 1948, bring the country to independence, to become the largest democracy in the world. Although it still has widespread poverty, a caste system, 'honour' killings and a rape culture, there is now a prosperous middle class, high-tech and knowledge industries which produce leading research, a situation unforeseeable in the nineteenth century. Dalits, the former untouchables, have greater access to education, albeit with inadequate support, and inroads have been made on attitudes to rape. Corruption in government remains serious, but elections are held and governments change.

Nightingale's role in reform in India has been outlined in Chapter 6, with her move from top-down, official-driven reforms to the promotion of the efforts of Indian nationals and their organizations. She influenced progressive officials to be more ambitious in their goals. It took independence, however, to stop the 'drain' of resources, in Dadabhai Naoroji's terms, whereby British officials took their salaries and pensions out of the country, their very holding of the top positions necessarily denying them to Indians.

It took independence, too, to end the acceptance of famine. The failure of the British government to prevent or alleviate massive famines eventually provoked recourse to political solutions. When the Conservative Lord Lytton dismissed Allan Octavian Hume, his (Liberal) Agriculture Minister, and son of a radical MP, Hume went on to become a co-founder of the Indian National Congress, which led the struggle for self-government until independence was achieved in 1948. Famines continued long after Nightingale retired from active work. William Wedderburn, Lord Ripon and other friends continued to work to alleviate them. The Indian Famine Union was formed in London in 1901, to argue for flexibility in collecting debts in stricken areas, agricultural banks and loans.

Indian reformers realized that they had to organize both on famine and democratic reform, and they understood the connection between the two. The Nobel laureate Amartya Sen explained in his 1999 book that democracy and political rights could even help to prevent famine:

Authoritarian rulers, who are themselves rarely affected by famines (or other such economic calamities), tend to lack the incentive to take timely preventive measures. Democratic governments, in contrast, have to win elections and face public criticism, and have strong incentives to undertake measures to avert famines and other such catastrophes. It is not surprising that no famine has ever taken place in the history of the world in a functioning democracy.[14]

11

Health, healing and the environment

Nightingale's positive definition of health would become widely accepted, not only in nursing but in the health sciences generally. Her final definition of the word, given in an article in Quain's *Dictionary of Medicine* (1883), is: 'Health is not only to be well, but to be able to use well every power we have to use.'[1] It would be echoed in the definition given at the founding of the World Health Organization in 1948: 'Health is a state of complete physical, mental and social well-being and not merely the absence of disease or infirmity.'

Nightingale's emphasis on the prevention, rather than merely the cure, of disease made particular sense in her day, when effective drugs and other treatments were scarce and epidemics killed people in large numbers. When her advice was sought on an impending cholera epidemic in 1884 in the United States, she sent a letter to the editor of the *New York Herald*, with instructions on the necessity to remove filth and cleanse water, and it was reprinted in both a British and an American public health journal.[2] The irate writer of a letter to a newspaper in Tasmania attached a copy of it, along with pointed reference to the 'disgraceful . . . swamp' of Launceston, Tasmania.[3] When a cholera epidemic threatened again in 1892, Nightingale's advice was reprinted in *The Times* and other papers, and issued as a pamphlet.[4]

As nursing became an academic discipline, and professors began to publish theories of nursing, Nightingale would typically be mentioned as the first theorist, for her environmental theory. Nightingale heads a list of 24 theorists in one textbook.[5] 'Holistic nurses' still pay attention to surrounding biophysical factors in the way put forward by Nightingale, but few others do. Later theorists have perhaps assumed that hospital administrators will take care of environmental defects, so that nurses need not concern themselves with such matters.

Nightingale's belief that nurses should be patients' advocates has similarly been sidelined in contemporary nursing. When scandals over gross patient neglect emerge, however, the investigators muse about what Nightingale would have said. In the case of the excessive numbers of deaths at Stafford Hospital in the UK in 2005–8, the chair of the public inquiry, Robert Francis, QC, echoed her statement in *Notes on Hospitals*: 'It may seem a strange principle to enunciate as the very first requirement in a hospital that it should do the sick no harm. Unfortunately this requirement has not been met at Stafford Hospital.'[6]

Environmental principles applied to hospitals

Nightingale's decades of work to make hospitals safer, by paying attention to the environmental factors that make for disease, eventually paid off. The pavilion hospital she and her allies favoured became the dominant model around the world in the second half of the nineteenth century. Fine pavilion hospitals such as the Leeds General Infirmary, the Edinburgh Royal Infirmary and the Royal Victoria Hospital in Montreal became tourist sites. Some hospital planners even called the pavilion model a 'Nightingale hospital'. Although they used her published material without direct, personal contact, the New York Board of Commissioners did the same when building an emigrant hospital on Ward's Island in 1863.[7]

The 'Nightingale ward', the long, narrow ward – or pavilion – with facing windows, became the standard nursing unit. 'From 1861 to the beginning of World War II, the Nightingale ward was the dominant accommodation in Britain, indeed very nearly the only available design for a nursing unit.'[8] That design was favoured for ease of supervision as well as hygiene.

Among the many countries to take up the pavilion model was Australia, where, in an article on hospital repairs, the principle was described as 'strongly advocated by Miss Nightingale'.[9] In 1874, a new wing for another Australian hospital was said to have been built according to her principles, with details given on cubic space and ward size,[10] while her work was cited in 1886 when a new hospital was under consideration in Melbourne.[11]

In an article published in *Chambers' Encyclopaedia* in 1890, Nightingale was as firm as ever on her preference for the pavilion model; ideally it should have only one floor, two were admissible, three 'insanitary'. Furthermore, she stated that no more than 100 patients should ever be housed under the same roof.[12]

The pavilion ward worked well in the years before the discovery of penicillin and other antibiotics. Once these became widely available, patients needed to stay in hospital for shorter periods and the need for the ward sister to be able to observe patients for the duration of fever crises declined. Improvements in artificial ventilation and heating made cross-ventilation by means of open windows less necessary, even undesirable in extreme climates. The high cost of land was another factor pushing hospitals towards high-rise configurations.

Having been bombed badly in the Second World War, St Thomas's Hospital was rebuilt in line with post-war practice after it; its new high-rise buildings were air conditioned. Three of its old pavilions remain, reconfigured later for offices and day clinics. Interestingly, when the Chief Architect of the Department of Health was hospitalized there in one of the old pavilions, he was surprised to discover that he liked it, and that doctors, nurses and patients preferred it too. An empirical survey subsequently confirmed that the pavilion design was indeed favoured, in practice, by all three groups.[13]

Queen Alexandra's Military Hospital, Millbank, was one of the last general military hospitals to be built on the pavilion principle in the UK. It opened in 1905, closing only in the 1970s. Architects, moreover, continue to recognize Nightingale's influence on hospital design, and especially on that of military hospitals. Her ideas 'set the standard . . . against which the performance – functionally or otherwise – of all hospitals would be judged to a great extent until the outbreak of World War 2'.

Her ward prototype emphasized 'cleanliness, hygiene, ambiance and functional efficiency'. Her hospital advice 'was scientifically verifiable, and the day-lit naturally ventilated, narrow, open pavilion was ideal for this new understanding of infection and disease control'.[14] She was also the 'first modern practitioner of evidence-based research and development'.[15]

Comparative statistics on hospital mortality are not available, so that no firm assessment can be made of the success of the pavilion model. Moreover, improvements took time, and many old hospital buildings still stood, so that it was not until late in the nineteenth century that hospitals had become somewhat safer places. Abel-Smith was circumspect in saying that patients could in that era 'be reasonably certain of dying from the disease with which they were admitted', meaning, at last, that they would not succumb to one acquired in hospital.[16] Clearly, the death rate among those admitted dropped significantly from the 10 per cent that was standard among London teaching hospitals in 1860.

The continuing threat of hospital-acquired infections

In Nightingale's day, 'hospitalism', 'hospital disease' and 'hospital atmosphere' were the terms used to refer to diseases caught in hospital by cross-infection, which the pavilion model was designed to prevent. With antibiotics, patients who pick up such an infection can normally be treated successfully.

However, diseases resistant to antibiotics, such as C-difficile, SARS, MRSA and Ebola, continue to evolve. In the twenty-first century, the threat of hospital-acquired infections has led to greater use of single-bed rooms and facilities for isolating hospital sections at the start of an outbreak. The standardization of washing facilities – which are always placed on the same side of the patient – is thought to encourage routine handwashing before the next patient is treated.

National health data shows that hospital-acquired infections are still common. The US Centers for Disease Control and Prevention estimated, from a sample of 165 acute-care

American hospitals, that about 1 in 25 patients got at least one 'healthcare-associated infection' in hospital, with about 75,000 patients dying from them in 2011.[17] In the UK, the National Institute for Health and Care Excellence, when issuing new guidelines on basic hygiene, estimated that 300,000 patients every year develop an infection while being treated by the NHS.[18] In Canada it has been estimated that, in a population roughly one-tenth of the USA and one-third of the UK, more than 200,000 patients got infections in hospitals, and some 8,000 died.[19]

Nightingale's effective use of outcomes data, at a time when the science was limited, and her advice on the careful monitoring of new treatments, remain sound advice. The prudent healthcare planner cannot assume that antidotes to new, resistant strains of pathogens will be found quickly, if at all.

Rediscovering sunlight and gardens

'No child can be well who is not bright and merry and brought up in fresh air and sunshine and surrounded by love – the sunshine of the soul.'[20] Abandonment of the pavilion model in favour of high-rises entailed the loss of outside space, for the old pavilions had gardens between them. Indeed, hospital gardens more generally fell out of favour during the twentieth century. One author noted that, when the roof garden at a San Francisco hospital was removed, the now bare space became a spot for staff to take a cigarette break.[21] From 1950 to 1990, according to land-scape architects, the 'therapeutic value of access to nature all but disappeared from hospitals in most western countries' in favour of air-conditioned high-rises.

While the pavilion model gave way to high-rise hospitals during much of the twentieth century, however, Nightingale's ideas on sunlight and gardens began to come back into favour late in the century, and the trend continues. Her emphasis on sunlight as a healing agent has found new support in the emerging field of neuroplasticity. From *Notes on Nursing* on, she insisted that sunlight was second only to fresh air as an essential of healing. This focus also reflects her basic philosophy that held healing to be a natural process, in which the nurse and doctor should remove obstructions and provide the conditions – including lots of sunlight – for the person to heal.

The psychiatrist Norman Doidge has credited Nightingale both with this early insight into the importance of sunlight, and with the leadership that ensured its acceptance in hospital design.[22] He, and others, acknowledge that while sunlight was recognized as a healing agent by the ancient Egyptians and Romans (Nightingale herself, incidentally, was overwhelmed by sunlight during her visit to Egypt in 1849–50), she was the first to apply it to hospital design.

Electric lightbulbs, erroneously thought to have the same spectrum as sunlight, replaced natural light in hospitals because, said Doidge, 'science could not explain Nightingale's insight that sunlight actually heals.' He especially liked her metaphor of sunlight acting not only as a painter, but a 'sculptor', that it could 'sculpt the circuitry of the brain'.[23]

The trend was reversed in the 1990s in the United States, triggered by the patient-centred care movement.[24] A model development at a Toronto hospital, for a new 'Patient Care Centre' announced in 2015, notes an increased number of single rooms, units that can be converted easily for isolation in case of an outbreak, plus 'large lawn areas, a roof garden for patients, visitors and staff'.[25] Consumer surveys show that patients, especially those with depression, prefer gardens, views, balconies and indoor plants.[26] Nightingale's ideas, in short, are making a comeback. Gardens might indeed be the place to bring her name back into the hospital system. Now that 'Nightingale wards' have gone, and the value of greenery and flowers been rediscovered, why not 'Nightingale gardens'?

12

Research, policy and legacy

From research methods to policy formation

Nightingale grounded her approach to research on classic sources, notably John Stuart Mill's *System of Logic* and L. A. J. Quetelet's *Physique sociale*. She not only produced good research herself, but remains a model both on the conduct of research and its use in policy formation.

Reports are not 'self-executive', Nightingale used to remind her colleagues. Action on policy recommendations could not be left to good luck; a strategy was required to build support for them. Typically, the first stage was the organization of favourable reviews in leading journals by respected, sympathetic persons. Questions in Parliament and newspaper coverage had to be managed. All this would become mainstream practice in the twentieth century, and would be taught in universities and colleges.

Nightingale never set out a specific methodology for the process, but a strategy and sequence are clear in what she and her colleagues did:

- the formulation of research questions;
- a review of the literature. Here she emphasized the use of official reports and government documents, primary sources, not 'magaziney articles', as she called much commentary;

- interviews with report writers, where possible. She debriefed officials on their work, a procedure obviously not available to everyone, but highly useful for gaining context;
- consultation with practitioners, those who would use the research when it was completed;
- the pre-testing of questionnaires, on small numbers of respondents, to ensure clarity of wording (Nightingale's questionnaires were sent to institutions, not individuals, but the principle holds).

After the research was completed and the data had received a preliminary analysis, the following steps were taken:

- further consultation with experts, particularly those expected to use them, on the interpretation of results;
- recommendations for improvements in the areas concerned were made, again based on consultation;
- a media-relations strategy was implemented to promote the report and its recommendations.

The last of these required knowledge of the relevant newspapers and journals, their circulation and their editors; getting the right person to review a report for the right journal could give it a better chance. Briefings with sympathetic MPs had to be arranged. Nightingale often had her reports reprinted for separate circulation, apart from any given by the organization in question.

All these tasks would seem obvious today, but had to be learned step by step in hers. Policy courses leading to positions such as senior policy advisor are now taught in professional schools. There are careers in the formulation and advocacy of policy, in government and non-governmental organizations and in media relations. Major nursing organizations employ people to develop policy for advocacy, on healthcare in broad terms and now on the environment. Some – the Ontario Registered Nurses Association, for example – have excellent statements on climate change.

The Nightingale legacy

But how important was Nightingale's work to the great reform movements of the nineteenth century? She always worked with colleagues, and sometimes followed earlier pioneers, so that the question must be asked as to what difference she herself made.

In the creation of the modern nursing profession, the evidence is overwhelming that she made the greatest possible difference. Not only did her Crimean War fund pay for the first training schools, it was Nightingale's vision that shaped them. Earlier women, notably Elizabeth Fry, had contributed to the modest amount of training given to women to become private nurses, and two matrons, Sarah Wardroper and Mary Jones, brought in higher standards of nursing at their own hospitals; neither, however, aspired either to founding a training school or to routinely staffing hospitals with trained nurses. Nightingale did, and for decades she led the work that achieved those goals.

On workhouse nursing and the eventual demolition of the Poor Law, Nightingale's work was again vital, although colleagues contributed significantly; William Rathbone notably funded the first experiment in Liverpool, Agnes Jones led the nursing there, and many 'workhouse doctors' made important contributions. Nightingale, however, always had the boldest vision, articulated it clearly, and encouraged others to be more ambitious in their goals.

Nightingale is no longer given much recognition for any of this in the nursing profession in the UK and other western countries. Her ideas on ethics, best practice and health promotion are taught without acknowledgement that they came from her. Nurses trained in many institutions graduate without ever hearing of her. Yet an introduction to her basic *Notes on Nursing* would still be helpful for undergraduate nurses, while graduate students would benefit from study of her more advanced writing.

Nightingale's legacy in the field of hospital safety, one shared with important colleagues, is better recognized. She could not have managed the technical demands without the collaboration of doctors (John Sutherland and John Roberton), architects (George Godwin and numerous others) and engineers (Douglas Galton and Robert Rawlinson). Yet all of them deferred to her on her ambitious vision, relished the encouragement she gave to their joint projects and, thanks to that encouragement, undoubtedly went further in their aspirations than they ever would have done alone. Recent analysts of hospital reform give her the credit for the widespread acceptance of the pavilion model.[1] The methods Nightingale used in her work, with regard to both nursing and hospitals, are now mainstream, under the term 'evidence-based health care'.

As regards improvements to the status of women, Nightingale was a valued supporter rather than the initiator. Her name counted in the suffrage movement at a time of so much opposition, but major credit is also due to John Stuart Mill, Mentia Taylor, Millicent Fawcett and their suffrage organizations. Nightingale also gave support to women's struggle for access to higher education and for the granting of property rights, although her contribution here was again short of pivotal.

As to reform in India, a matter to which Nightingale gave so much of her time and energy for 40 years, there is little for which her work can be seen to have been crucial, beyond getting the Royal Commission on India established. She did solid research for the Commission, then worked assiduously on implementing its recommendations. However, its focus was military and the reforms so desperately needed by Indian nationals themselves, especially the poorest, were slow and partial. The country's great advances to self-government, independence and prosperity did not occur until after her lifetime. But she deserves credit for producing excellent material and encouraging two generations of Indian leaders.

Finally, her great motivator – her devout Christian faith – can be seen to have been important, and her views – including a great respect for other faiths – might win more favour today if there were any identifiable school or theory to carry them forward. In the twentieth century, however, Christian nurses did begin forming new organizations to bring their faith and work together. A Nurses Christian Movement was established in Melbourne, Australia, in 1913, and soon became a national body. Similar Nurses Christian Fellowship groups date from the 1930s in the United States, Canada and Scotland, and they have spread to India, Japan, the Philippines, Singapore and other countries. These groups subsequently amalgamated with the evangelical Inter-Varsity Christian Fellowship, which serves university students. The Nurses Christian Fellowship International dates from 1962. A New Zealand group re-formed in 2015, on Nightingale's birthday.

Nightingale's bicentenary

Doubtless the bicentenary of Florence Nightingale's birth in 2020 will prompt new reassessments of her legacy and its ongoing relevance. It is hoped that this 'brief history' will provide food for thought. Jaded nursing professionals may find here a powerful source of encouragement in the challenges they face by examining how she met and solved the problems of her day.

Finally, it seems that the time is long past for describing Nightingale as a 'great Victorian' or 'the greatest woman' of her time. The scope and lasting power of her ideas and achievements go beyond her gender and her era.

Disease has still to be confronted and overcome – or, better still, prevented – by sturdy measures for health promotion, but her work in this field remains a precious resource. So too can reformers working on so many issues of today, including the environment, gender and race inequality, war, famine and international development, find inspiration in her vision.

Notes

1 Nightingale and the nineteenth century

1 Unpublished essay in Lynn McDonald (ed.), *Florence Nightingale's Theology: Essays, Letters and Journal Notes* (Waterloo, ON: Wilfrid Laurier University Press, 2002), p. 94.

2 Letter 24 August 1863, in McDonald, *Nightingale's Theology*, pp. 367–8.

3 Jacob Abbott, *The Corner-stone, or, a Familiar Illustration of the Principles of Christian Truth* (London: T. Ward, 1834).

4 Letter 10 December 1895, in Lynn McDonald (ed.), *Florence Nightingale on Women: Medicine, Midwifery and Prostitution* (Waterloo, ON: Wilfrid Laurier University Press, 2005), p. 927.

5 Jacob Abbott, *The Way to Do Good, or the Christian Character Mature* (London: Tegg, 1836).

6 Letter 24 November [1849], in Gérard Vallée (ed.), *Florence Nightingale on Mysticism and Eastern Religions* (Waterloo, ON: Wilfrid Laurier University Press, 2003), p. 155.

7 'Can We Educate Education in India', in Gérard Vallée (ed.), *Florence Nightingale on Social Change in India* (Waterloo, ON: Wilfrid Laurier University Press, 2007), p. 652.

8 Letter [July 1850], in Lynn McDonald (ed.), *Florence Nightingale's European Travels* (Waterloo, ON: Wilfrid Laurier University Press, 2004), pp. 449–50.

9 Letter 19 April 1889, in McDonald, *Nightingale's European Travels*, p. 345.

10 Letter 29 August [1852] in McDonald, *Nightingale's European Travels*, p. 712.

11 Letter 24 November [1849], in Vallée, *Nightingale on Mysticism and Eastern Religions*, p. 157.

2 Faith in a secular world

1 Note 25 March 1872, in Lynn McDonald (ed.), *Florence Nightingale's Theology: Essays, Letters and Journal Notes* (Waterloo, ON: Wilfrid Laurier University Press, 2002), p. 159.

2 Letter 18 September 1892, in McDonald, *Nightingale's Theology*, p. 240.

3 Herder, *Vom Geist der Hebräischen Poesie*, in Lynn McDonald (ed.), *Florence Nightingale's Spiritual Journey: Biblical Annotations, Sermons and Journal Notes* (Waterloo, ON: Wilfrid Laurier University Press, 2001).

4 Note, British Library Add Mss 45784, f43.

5 In Gérard Vallée (ed.), *Florence Nightingale on Mysticism and Eastern Religions* (Waterloo, ON: Wilfrid Laurier University Press, 2003), pp. 17–80.

6 Evelyn Underhill, *Practical Mysticism: A Little Book for Normal People* (New York: E. P. Dutton, 1915), p. 65.

7 'The Livingstone Expedition', *The Times*, 31 January 1872, p. 8B.

8 Letter to Agnes Livingstone, 18 February 1874, in Lynn McDonald (ed.), *Florence Nightingale on Society and Politics, Philosophy, Science, Education and Literature* (Waterloo, ON: Wilfrid Laurier University Press, 2003), pp. 538–9.

9 Letter 17 December 1885, in Gérard Vallée (ed.), *Florence Nightingale on Social Change in India* (Waterloo, ON: Wilfrid Laurier University Press, 2007), p. 739.

10 Letter 9 May 1879, in Vallée, *Nightingale on Social Change in India*, p. 725.

11 Letter 24 November [1849], in Vallée, *Nightingale on Mysticism and Eastern Religions*, p. 155.

12 Note, 5 July 1898, in Vallée, *Nightingale on Social Change in India*, pp. 876–7.

13 Letter 7 May 1870, in McDonald, *Nightingale's Theology*, pp. 389–90.

14 Nightingale, 'Una and the Lion', in Lynn McDonald (ed.), *Florence Nightingale on Public Health Care* (Waterloo, ON: Wilfrid Laurier University Press, 2004), p. 301.

15 Letter 4 November 1870, in McDonald, *Nightingale on Public Health Care*, p. 443.

16 Letter 24 December 1877, American Nurses Association website.

17 Letter 3 November 1896, in Lynn McDonald (ed.), *Florence Nightingale and the Nightingale School* (Waterloo, ON: Wilfrid Laurier University Press, 2009), p. 489.

18 References here are given to the year of the address, available in two sources: Rosalind Nash (ed.), *Florence Nightingale to her Nurses: A Selection from Miss Nightingale's Addresses to Probationers and Nurses of the Nightingale School at St Thomas's Hospital* (London: Macmillan, 1914), and McDonald, *Nightingale and the Nightingale School*, pp. 761–881.

19 Nightingale, 'Nursing the Sick', in McDonald, *Nightingale and the Nightingale School*, pp. 750–1.

20 Letter 21 December 1892, McGill University CUS 417/88.43.

21 Letter 31 January 1856, in McDonald, *Nightingale and the Nightingale School*, p. 119.

22 Letter *c.* 25 April 1846, in McDonald, *Nightingale's Theology*, p. 348.

23 Letter 17 September 1882, in Lynn McDonald (ed.), *Florence Nightingale on Wars and the War Office* (Waterloo, ON: Wilfrid Laurier University Press, 2011), p. 931.

24 Letter 7 June 1885, in Lynn McDonald (ed.), *Florence Nightingale: An Introduction to her Life and Family* (Waterloo, ON: Wilfrid Laurier University Press, 2002), p. 366.

25 Leo Gregory Fink, 'Catholic Influences in the Life of Florence Nightingale', St Louis, MO: Catholic Hospital Association Bulletin No. 19, p. 3.

26 Letter 25 October 1891, in McDonald, *Nightingale on Society and Politics*, p. 823.

27 Letter 12 May 1890, in McDonald, *Nightingale on Society and Politics*, p. 820.

3 The Crimean War

1 Nightingale's correspondence and reports on the war are extensively reported in Lynn McDonald (ed.), *Florence Nightingale and the Crimean War* (Waterloo, ON: Wilfrid Laurier University Press, 2010).

2 Cyrus Hamlin, *My Life and Times*, 2nd edn (Boston: Congregational Sunday School & Publishing Society, 1893), pp. 329–32.

3 Mary Seacole, *Wonderful Adventures of Mrs Seacole in Many Lands*, ed. W. J. S. (London: James Blackwood, 1857), p. 91. The incident has been strangely transmogrified in recent years to claim that Nightingale refused to hire Seacole as a nurse; a BBC 'educational' video even suggests that this was for reasons of racism. The Royal College of Nursing has made Seacole into Nightingale's equal as a pioneer nurse, without ever saying where or when she nursed. St Thomas's Hospital has welcomed a statue of Seacole on its site, and the Chancellor of the Exchequer found money for it. All of this suits a political correctness campaign, with no basis in primary-source fact. See Lynn McDonald, *Mary Seacole: The Making of the Myth* (Toronto: Iguana Books, 2014), pp. 11–12, 81, 194.

4 Florence Nightingale, *Notes on Matters Affecting the Health, Efficiency and Hospital Administration of the British Army*, much of it in McDonald, *Nightingale and the Crimean War*, pp. 575–888.

5 Florence Nightingale, 'Answers to Written Questions Addressed to Miss Nightingale by the Commissioners', and in McDonald, *Nightingale and the Crimean War*, pp. 889–972.

4 Founding a new profession

1 Robert James Graves, *A System of Clinical Medicine* (Dublin: Fannin, 1843), p. 60.

2 Letter 4 August 1883, British Library Add Mss 45775 f133.

3 A. Gawande, 'Notes of a Surgeon: On Washing Hands', *New England Journal of Medicine* 350 (2004), 1283–6.

4 Henry Bence-Jones, 'Report on the Accommodation in St Pancras Workhouse', *Accounts and Papers of the House of Commons* XLIX, p. 5.

5 Joseph Rogers, *Joseph Rogers, M.D.: Reminiscences of a Workhouse Medical Officer*, ed. Thorold Rogers (London: T. Fisher Unwin, 1889).

6 Ruth Richardson, 'Middlesex Hospital Outpatients/Strand Union Workhouse', *History Today* 43.9 (September 1993).

7 Letter to Edwin Chadwick 9 July 1866, in Lynn McDonald (ed.), *Florence Nightingale on Public Health Care* (Waterloo, ON: Wilfrid Laurier University Press, 2004), p. 347.

8 Letter [12 October 1867], in McDonald, *Nightingale on Public Health Care*, p. 432.

5 Safer hospitals

1 Jacques René Tenon, *Memoirs on Paris Hospitals*, ed. Dora B. Weiner (Canton, MA: Science History, 1996).

2 Letter 20 February 1864, *Medical Times and Gazette*, p. 211.

3 John D. Thompson and Grace Goldin, *The Hospital: A Social and Architectural History* (New Haven, CT: Yale University Press, 1975), p. 231.

4 Notes 17 January 1888, in Lynn McDonald (ed.), *Florence Nightingale and Hospital Reform* (Waterloo, ON: Wilfrid Laurier University Press, 2012), p. 894.

5 Florence Nightingale, *Notes on Hospitals*, 3rd edn (London: Longmans Green, 1863), ch. 6; McDonald, 'Hospitals', in *Nightingale and Hospital Reform*, p. 916.

6 Listed in McDonald, *Nightingale and Hospital Reform*, pp. 499–500.

7 Letter 19 April 1877, in McDonald, *Nightingale and Hospital Reform*, p. 823.

8 Jeremy Taylor, *The Architect and the Pavilion Hospital: Dialogue and Design Creativity in England 1850–1914* (London: Leicester University Press, 1997), p. 67.

9 Letter 23 January 1885, in Lynn McDonald (ed.), *Florence Nightingale and the Nightingale School* (Waterloo, ON: Wilfrid Laurier University Press, 2009), p. 379.

6 Promoting health and better conditions in India

1 Letter 6 August 1883, in Lynn McDonald (ed.), *Florence Nightingale on Society and Politics, Philosophy, Science, Education and Literature* (Waterloo, ON: Wilfrid Laurier University Press, 2003), pp. 425–6.

2 Lawrence letter 5 February 1864, British Library Add Mss 45777 f31.

3 Dadabhai Naoroji, *Poverty in India: Papers and Speeches of Dadabhai Naoroji* (London: Winckworth, Foulger & Aldine Press, 1888).

4 Nightingale, in D. Gidumal, *Behramji M. Malabari: A Biographical Sketch* (London: Fisher & Unwin, 1892).

5 Gérard Vallée (ed.), *Florence Nightingale on Health in India* (Waterloo, ON: Wilfrid Laurier University Press, 2006); *Florence Nightingale on Social Change in India* (Waterloo, ON: Wilfrid Laurier University Press, 2007).

6 Andrew Roberts, *Salisbury, Victorian Titan* (London: Weidenfeld & Nicolson, 1999), p. 85, in Vallée, *Nightingale on Health in India*, pp. 105–7.

7 Note 7 May 1888, in Vallée, *Nightingale on Health in India*, p. 934.

8 Report of the Famine Commission, Parliamentary Papers, 31May 1867, in Vallée, *Nightingale on Health in India*, pp. 704–5.

9 Mike Davis, *Late Victorian Holocausts: El Nino Famines and the Making of the Third World* (London: Verso, 2001).

10 William E. Gladstone, *Political Speeches in Scotland, November and December 1879* (Edinburgh: Andrew Elliot, 1879), p. 202.

11 Davis, *Late Victorian Holocausts*, p. 28.

12 Letter 20 October 1879, in Vallée, *Nightingale on Health in India*, p. 631.

13 Letter 4 January 1879, in Vallée, *Nightingale on Health in India*, p. 818.

14 Undated note, British Library Add Mss 45836 f230.

7 Army reform and later wars

1 Nightingale, 'Army Sanitary Administration', in Lynn McDonald (ed.), *Florence Nightingale on Wars and the War Office* (Waterloo, ON: Wilfrid Laurier University Press, 2011), p. 344.

2 Dr John Sutherland letter 22–3 March 1858, British Library Add Mss 45751 f55.

3 Beverly M. Calkins, 'Florence Nightingale: on Feeding an Army', *American Journal of Clinical Nutrition* 50 (1989), 1260–5.

4 Ann A. Hertzler, 'Florence Nightingale's Influence on Civil War Nutrition', *Nutrition Today* 39.4 (July–August 1997), pp. 157–8.

5 Charles Janeway Stillé, *History of the United States Sanitary Commission, Being the General Report of its Work during the War of the Rebellion* (Philadelphia, PA: J. B. Lippincott, 1866), p. 27.

6 William Rutherford, Diary. Private collection, Dollar, Scotland.

7 John F. Hutchison, *Champions of Charity: War and the Rise of the Red Cross* (Boulder, CO: Westview, 1996), pp. 350, 426.

8 Letter 11 November 1871, in McDonald, *Nightingale on Wars and the War Office*, p. 814.

9 Letter to *The Lancet* 96:2464 (19 November 1870), 725.

10 Letter 18 February 1879, in Lynn McDonald (ed.), *Florence Nightingale on Society and Politics, Philosophy, Science, Education and Literature* (Waterloo, ON: Wilfrid Laurier University Press, 2003), p. 324.

11 Letter 8 November 1881, in McDonald, *Nightingale on Wars and the War Office*, pp. 873–4.

12 Undated note, British Library Add Mss 45836 f211. For background, see McDonald, 'The Egyptian Campaigns', in *Nightingale on Wars and the War Office*, pp. 905–1019.

8 Nursing: the profession of patient care

1 Lynn McDonald (ed.), *Florence Nightingale on Extending Nursing* (Waterloo, ON: Wilfrid Laurier University Press, 2009).

2 McDonald, *Nightingale on Extending Nursing*, pp. 384–404.

3 Florence Nightingale, 'Health and Local Government', *Report of the Bucks Sanitary Conference October* (Aylesbury: Poulton, 1894), i–ii. In Lynn McDonald (ed.), *Nightingale on Public Health Care* (Waterloo, ON: Wilfrid Laurier University Press, 2004), p. 601.

4 Angelique Lucille Pringle, *A Study in Nursing* (London: Macmillan, 1905).

5 Fred Smith, *A Short History of the Royal Army Medical Corps* (Aldershot: Gale & Polden, 1929), pp. 11–14.

6 Letter of Grace R. Osler 11 November 1916, McGill University Osler Library, CUS 417/122.43.

7 Celia Davies, 'Making Sense of the Census in Britain and the U.S.A.: The Changing Occupational Classification and the Position of Nurses', *Sociological Review* 28.3 (1980), 581–609, at 595–6.

8 *World Health Statistics Report*, 2011.

9 Florence Nightingale, 'Method of Improving the Nursing Service of Hospitals', n.d. [1867].

10 Nightingale, 'Health and Local Government'.

9 The National Health Service

1 Brian Abel-Smith, *A History of the Nursing Profession* (London: Heinemann, 1960), p. 49.

2 Allyson M. Pollock and David Price, *Duty to Care: In Defence of Universal Health Care* (London: Centre for Labour and Social Studies, 2013), p. 5.

3 David Cecere, 'New Study Finds 45,000 Deaths Annually Linked to Lack of Health Coverage', *Harvard Gazette* online, 17 December 2009.

4 WHO, 'Health and Human Rights'. Fact Sheet no. 323 (December 2015).

10 Mainstream social and political reform

1 Lynn McDonald (ed.), *Florence Nightingale on Women: Medicine, Midwifery and Prostitution* (Waterloo: Wilfrid Laurier University Press, 2005), pp. 411–505.

2 Letter 20 March 1884, in Lynn McDonald (ed.), *Florence Nightingale on Society and Politics, Philosophy, Science, Education and Literature* (Waterloo: Wilfrid Laurier University Press, 2003), p. 137.

3 'The Higher Education of Women', *The Times*, 14 February 1878, p. 10E.

4 Letter 21 February 1874, in McDonald, *Nightingale on Women*, p. 783.

5 Brian Abel-Smith, *The Hospitals, 1800–1948: A Study in Social Administration in England and Wales* (London: Heinemann, 1964), p. 82.

6 Abel-Smith, *The Hospitals*, p. 76.

7 Brian Abel-Smith, *A History of the Nursing Profession* (London: Heinemann, 1960), p. 122.

8 Letter 9 July 1866, in Lynn McDonald (ed.), *Florence Nightingale on Public Health Care* (Waterloo: Wilfrid Laurier University Press, 2004), p. 346.

9 Letter 9 July 1866, in McDonald, *Nightingale on Public Health Care*, p. 347.

10 Nightingale, 'A Note on Pauperism', in McDonald, *Nightingale on Society and Politics*, p. 137.

11 Letter 11 February 1868, in McDonald, *Nightingale on Society and Politics*, p. 154.

12 William Beveridge, *Report of the Inter-Departmental Committee on Social Insurance and Allied Services* (London: HMSO, 1942), Cmnd 6404.

13 Letter [12 October 1867], in McDonald, *Nightingale on Public Health Care*, p. 432.

14 Amartya K. Sen, *Development as Freedom* (Oxford: Oxford University Press, 1999), p. 16.

11 Health, healing and the environment

1 Nightingale, 'Nursing the Sick', in Lynn McDonald (ed.), *Florence Nightingale and the Nightingale School* (Waterloo, ON: Wilfrid Laurier University Press, 2009), pp. 735–6.

2 'Practical Advice in View of the Rapid Spread of Cholera: "Scavenge, Scavenge, Scavenge"', *The Sanitarian* 13 (1884), pp. 114–15; 'Miss Florence Nightingale on the Cholera', *The Sanitary Record* 6.73 (1884), 66.

3 'Cholera in Launceston', *Daily Telegraph*, 16 October 1884, p. 3.

4 'The Cholera', *The Times*, 2 September 1892, p. 9D.

5 P. A. Potter et al. (eds), *Canadian Fundamentals of Nursing*, 2nd edn (Toronto: Mosby Elsevier, 2009), p. 95.

6 www.lexology.com/library/detail.aspx?g=fd341164-118c-4409-bb56-44978478258e.

7 New York Board of Commissioners, 'An Account of the Proceedings of the Laying of the Corner-stone of the State Emigrant Hospital'.

8 John D. Thompson and Grace Goldin, *The Hospital: A Social and Architectural History* (New Haven, CT: Yale University Press, 1975), p. 231.

9 'The Maitland Hospital', *Maitland Mercury and Hunter River General Advertiser*, 7 March 1868.

10 'Sandhurst Buildings in course of Erection', *Bendigo Advertiser*, 27 May 1874.

11 'The Melbourne Hospital', *Argus*, 19 May 1886.

12 Florence Nightingale, 'Hospitals', in *Chambers' Encyclopaedia* vol. 5, pp. 805–7; Lynn McDonald (ed.), *Florence Nightingale and Hospital Reform* (Waterloo, ON: Wilfrid Laurier University Press, 2012), p. 913.

13 Mike Nightingale, 'Buildings Update: Part 2: Evolving Wards', *Architecture Journal* (28 July 1982), 47–50, 54–61, at 48.

14 Stephen Verderber, *Innovations in Hospital Architecture* (New York: Routledge, 2010), pp. 22–5.

15 Stephen Verderber, *Compassion in Architecture: Evidence-based Design for Health in Louisiana* (Lafayette, LA: Center for Louisiana Studies, 2005), p. 177.

16 Brian Abel-Smith, *The Hospitals, 1800–1948: A Study in Social Administration in England and Wales* (London: Heinemann, 1964), p. 125.

17 Shelley S. Magill et al., 'Multistate Point-Prevalence Survey of Health Care-Associated Infections', *New England Journal of Medicine* 370 (March 2014), 1198–1208. Accessed August 2015.

18 'Hospital Infection Rates Must come Down, Says Watchdog', BBC Online, 17 April 2014.

19 Public Health Agency of Canada.

20 Nightingale, 'Rural Hygiene', Official Report of the Central Conference of Women Workers (Leeds, 1894), 46–60.

21 Clare Cooper Marcus and Marna Barnes (eds), *Healing Gardens: Therapeutic Benefits and Design Recommendations* (New York: John Wiley, 1999), p. 13.

22 Norman Doidge, 'Rewiring a Brain with Light', ch. 4 of *The Brain's Way of Healing: Remarkable Discoveries and Recoveries from the Frontiers of Neuroplasticity* (London: Penguin, 2015).

23 Doidge, *The Brain's Way of Healing*, p. 121.

24 Marcus and Barnes, *Healing Gardens*, p. 3.

25 Toronto East General Hospital Foundation, News Release, 24 February 2015.

26 Clare Cooper Marcus, 'Healing Gardens in Hospitals', *Interdisciplinary Design and Research eJournal* 1:1 (January 2007), p. 1.

12 Research, policy and legacy

 1 John D. Thompson and Grace Goldin, *The Hospital: A Social and Architectural History* (New Haven, CT: Yale University Press, 1975), p. 231; Jeremy Taylor, *Hospital and Asylum Architecture in England 1840–1914: Building for Health Care* (London: Mansell, 1991); James Stevens Curl, *Victorian Architecture: Diversity and Invention* (Reading: Spire Books, 2007), p. 479.

Further reading

Bostridge, Mark, *Florence Nightingale: The Making of an Icon* (London: Viking, 2008).

Dossey, Barbara M., *Florence Nightingale: Mystic, Visionary and Healer* (Philadelphia, PA: Springhouse, 1999).

Goldie, Sue M. (ed.), *'I Have Done my Duty': Florence Nightingale in the Crimean War 1854–1856* (Manchester: Manchester University Press, 1987).

McDonald, Lynn, *Florence Nightingale at First Hand* (London: Continuum/Bloomsbury, 2014).

Nightingale, Florence, *Notes on Nursing*, rev. edn (1860 or 1861).

Nightingale, Florence, *Notes on Hospitals*, 3rd edn (London: Longmans, Green, 1863).

Index

Index

Index

Index

Index

United States 36, 71, 72, 74–5,
    82, 94, 100, 106, 114; *see also*
    American Civil War, United
    States Sanitary Commission
United States Sanitary
    Commission 62, 114
universal health care 81, 83–4

ventilation 27, 34, 40–2, 96–7
Verney, Frederick 73
Verney, Lady Parthenope (née
    Nightingale) 8
Verney, Maude 7
Verney, Sir Harry 8
Victoria, Queen xiii, 12, 29, 35,
    47, 51, 53, 56, 64
Villiers, C. P. 90

War Office (UK) 25, 28–9, 63,
    110, 114–15
Wardroper, Sarah E. 32–3, 104
Webb, Beatrice and Sidney 89, 91
Wedderburn, Sir William 51, 93

welfare state 9, 84, 87–91
Wellington, Duke of 25
Wesley, John 14–15
Wilberforce, William 4
Wilhelm I, Kaiser 64
Wolseley, General Garnet 66
women: as doctors 78, 87, 108;
    education of 8, 16, 77, 86–7;
    Indian xv, 16, 87; property
    rights of 8, 86; status of 35,
    84, 86–7, 105; vote of 8, 86,
    105
workhouse infirmaries 36–9,
    42, 88; Chorlton 80–1;
    Holborn 37; Liverpool xiv,
    18; St Marylebone 43, 81; St
    Pancras (Highgate) 18, 37, 42,
    80; Shoreditch 80
World Health Organization 75,
    83, 94, 115
Wren, Christopher 41

Zenana mission 16